How to Invest in Real Estate with Your IRA and 401(k) and Pay Little or No Taxes

How to Invest in Real Estate with Your IRA and 401(k) and Pay Little or No Taxes

Turn Your Retirement Accounts into Wealth-Building Machines!

Hubert Bromma

McGraw-Hill

New York   Chicago   San Francisco   Lisbon   London
Madrid   Mexico City   Milan   New Delhi   San Juan
Seoul   Singapore   Sydney   Toronto

The *McGraw-Hill* Companies

1 2 3 4 5 6 7 8 9 0 DOC/DOC 0 9 8 7 6

ISBN-13   978-0-07-147167-1
ISBN-10   0-07-147167-7

This publication is designed to provide accurate and authoritative information in regard to the subject matter covered. It is sold with the understanding that neither the author nor the publisher is engaged in rendering legal, accounting, or other professional service. If legal advice or other expert assistance is required, the services of a competent professional person should be sought.

> —*From a Declaration of Principles jointly adopted by Committee of the American Bar Association and a Committee of Publishers.*

McGraw-Hill books are available at special quantity discounts to use as premiums and sales promotions, or for use in corporate training programs. For more information, please write to the Director of Special Sales, McGraw-Hill Professional, Two Penn Plaza, New York, NY 10121-2298. Or contact your local bookstore.

Contents

Preface

Investing in real estate as a means of acquiring wealth has been popular since the beginning of recorded history; however, many savvy investors are not aware that they can use their retirement plans to invest in real estate. Many people feel "trapped" in their stock market investments owing to common misconceptions about the types of investments that are permitted within individual retirement accounts (IRAs) and other retirement plans.

The widespread misconception that permissible IRA investments are limited to stocks, bonds, mutual funds, and certificates of deposits is the result of people and companies who are in the business of selling these products. The Internal Revenue Service (IRS) requires that you have an approved custodian for your IRA or other retirement plan. For the vast majority of investors, the custodian is a bank, brokerage firm, or mutual-fund company—the very companies that are in the business of selling investment products. These custodians simply choose to limit your IRA investment choices to the products they sell. These limits are not imposed by the IRS.

In fact, the only investment types that are prohibited by the IRS rules are life insurance and collectibles, such as artwork and antiques. The IRS rules allow you to invest your retirement funds in real estate, lend your IRA as a mortgage loan, and many other investment alternatives. The key is to have a custodian that is willing to allow you to self-direct your retirement plans, thereby expanding your investment choices and allowing you to freely choose how to direct your portfolio.

Since 1975, you could use Keogh plans (now called *qualified plans*) to purchase real estate, offering tax-deferred investment opportunities. Since then, IRAs have become popular because the contribution limits for simplified employee pension plans have increased. In 1997, Roth IRAs made tax-free investments phenomenally popular. And most recently, in 2006, Roth 401(k)s, which have no salary caps for deferrals, expand your options in investing. If your current plan doesn't allow you to take advantage of the broad investment possibilities, don't worry. You can easily transfer any non-self-directed IRA to a self-directed one or amend and restate an existing qualified plan to one that permits self-direction.

Whether you currently have retirement funds or are considering the benefits of setting funds aside specifically for retirement purposes, this book helps you assess which options are best for you. The methodology is straightforward and similar to performing a real estate transaction with nonretirement funds. Real examples give you a glimpse of the common types of transactions you can perform and creative ways to partner with your funds, as well as things to avoid. You'll also journey through the different kinds of retirement arrangements that are available and how to open and fund self-directed accounts. By understanding the mechanics, you will make sound real estate transactions and mitigate the tax consequences. When you direct your IRA and 401(k) to invest in real estate, it is important to ensure that you do not lose the tax advantages available because of violation of the IRS Code, so we've included material to assist you in making the right decisions.

As with any investment, there are pros and cons, depending on your personal circumstances and goals. For more than 30 years, the advantage of tax-deferred investing has been available to everyone who earns income. As self-directed plans become more popular and the tax laws become more sophisticated, the wise investor measures each situation carefully to see whether it's the right approach. In that regard, I strongly suggest that you use a local professional familiar with the investments you make, along with your professional team of administrators, advisors, attorneys, financial planners, and accountants, to help you to make the best decisions.

How to Invest in Real Estate with Your IRA and 401(k) and Pay Little or No Taxes

1

Getting Started

Real estate can offer increased returns, lower risk, and greater cash flow (especially important when you are ready to start taking distributions), or simply just a means for diversification. With a self-directed individual retirement account (IRA) or other retirement plan, you can invest in rental property, rehabs, commercial property, raw land, preconstruction contracts, lease purchases, bank notes, and other forms of real estate. Once you have identified a truly self-directed custodian or administrator, the process is very simple.

First, you need to establish the account and transfer or roll over funds from your existing retirement plans. Next, you find a piece of real estate or other investment that you would like to purchase in your IRA. Finally, you direct your administrator to purchase the property *within* your IRA account. This final point is essential and is what allows you to avoid or defer paying taxes on all the income and gains on the property. You are not taking a taxable distribution *from* your IRA; you are simply making an investment *within* your IRA, just like you do with mutual funds. All the income from the investment goes back into your IRA, and all the expenses of the property are paid from the IRA. You find the property, you make all the decisions, and your IRA reaps all the benefits!

Investing in real estate does not have to be any more difficult than investing in stocks or mutual funds. Risk is inherent in any investment. Evaluating the risk is a matter of either educating oneself about the market or hiring a trusted individual to provide the best advice available. Many of us don't investigate the inner workings of a large corporation before we purchase a stock but trust a broker to assess the investment. With real estate, you can get inspections and work with those who know the local market.

The opportunity to invest tax-deferred, or even tax-free, through your retirement plan comes with some restrictions. The purpose of these accounts is to save for your retirement, not to use them for a current benefit. A current benefit would include using a property owned by your IRA as a vacation or second home. In addition, it is prohibited for your IRA to buy property from, sell or lease property to, or extend a loan to you or any disqualified person. Disqualified persons include you, your children, your parents, your spouse, and any business or trust owned or controlled by these people.

Cash flow and appreciation are two of the most common reasons for people to invest in real estate. So how do you take the benefits of investing in real estate and combine them with your retirement goals? There are numerous ways to approach this, depending on the amount you have to invest, your comfort with risk, and your personal experience in the real estate arena. Here are some things we will explore:

Invest in real property directly. Use your retirement funds to invest in a property directly, be it a single-family home or an apartment complex. If you see a property coming on the market that you feel will appreciate, buy it with your IRA.

Use other people's IRAs or money. Combine your IRA with other people's IRAs or personal funds. This is a good method to use to make larger purchases, such as an apartment complex, or a single purchase of a dollar amount that exceeds your retirement fund. Each investor receives an undivided interest in the property, and all income is allocated directly in relationship to the amount invested by each person or IRA. You can even include family members as long as the transaction closes simultaneously.

Leverage the investment. You can have leveraged property in your retirement account. The loan must be nonrecourse to you as an individual. Some community banks and savings associations that are portfolio lenders make nonrecourse loans on investment properties. There may be a tax on the income on the amount financed, but this still can be an advantageous and worthwhile option.

Set up limited-liability companies (LLCs) or land trusts. Your IRA or plan can own interests in limited-liability companies or be a beneficiary of land trusts. These entities then can purchase investment properties.

Be a lender. Your retirement plan can lend to anyone who isn't your ascendant, descendant, or spouse of one of them. The loans can be long- or short-term or construction loans.

In all cases, all income, such as rents, goes into your retirement account, and all expenses, such as property management, maintenance, and marketing fees, are paid from your account.

The Hard Reality

In the United States, people are not saving for their retirement as they should. The savings rates for European and Japanese workers is about 10 to 15 percent, compared with American workers, who had negative savings in 2006. Although it's becoming more popular for employers to offer salary-deferred retirement plans, many employees do not take full or even partial advantage of the ability to put money aside for retirement. The negative savings rate and the lack of financial preparation for retirement will result in a national crisis over the next 10 years unless there is a cultural shift regarding retirement planning. In addition, the need for retirement funds is getting closer for baby boomers because the first wave reaches age 60 in 2006.

Let's look at this major demographic and what the next 10 to 20 years could bring. Baby boomers are those individuals born between 1946 and 1964. The average baby boomer is about 51 years old, has $35,000 in total household personal retirement savings, and typically saves $2,750 annually for retirement. In 15 years, at age 66, this adds up to only $41,250 (assuming no growth or interest). Those who defer funds to a 401(k) have an average account balance of $80,000. At this rate of savings, most of us will not have enough to retire. For some people, retirement funds may be the largest or only source of investment capital. Investing in real estate, with profits not taxed until taken as a distribution or never taxed in the case of Roth IRAs and Roth 401(k)s, may be an ideal way to maximize growth and ensure a more comfortable retirement.

For many of us, money for retirement is not our only future financial concern. Paying medical bills and college tuition can take a big chunk of our savings. But these, too, can be funded from accounts that operate in a similar fashion to IRAs, which can be self-directed to maximize their earning potential.

Now is as good a time as any to assess what your family's financial goals are and your options to save. Which retirement plan best fits your needs? Are you saving enough money for your child's college education? Will you have more money or less when you retire? To determine which type of plan is best for you, you need to figure out how much you can afford to contribute toward your plan based on your current financial situation. If the amount you can afford is $4,000 or less, a traditional or Roth IRA would make the most sense. These accounts are easy and inexpensive to set up. Traditional IRAs allow you to make pretax contributions, whereas Roth IRAs are after-tax contributions. Roth IRAs have annual income limitations that make you ineligible for annual contributions if you make too much money, and they are also taxed differently than traditional IRAs. Does your company offer a 401(k)? If so, how much can you afford to set aside each month? Will your company match some of your contributions? If so, taking full advantage of this is basically like getting free money.

If you are self-employed, you can choose from a longer list of retirement plans, such as simplified employee pension (SEP) IRAs, SIMPLE IRAs, individual

401(k)s, and profit-sharing plans. The main advantage of these kinds of plans is that they have higher contribution limits. Therefore, if your annual budget allows you to save more than $4,000 a year, you should consider establishing one of these plans.

Planning ahead is the most essential part of deciding which kind of tax-advantaged plan to use. Each option has different characteristics and qualification issues. These are covered in Chapter 2.

Once you have made the decision to use a tax-deferred or tax-free plan for real estate and real estate–related investments, you are ready to explore how to invest in real estate using your retirement plan. Investing in real estate or real estate–related assets is not limited to those who have huge retirement accounts. Whether you start with a $10,000 IRA or a $500,000 deferred retirement plan, there are opportunities for everyone. Let's quickly look at three scenarios.

Joel Starts Small

As real estate prices have continued to escalate, it has become more difficult to purchase a piece of property outright. If you have less than $25,000, one possibility is to loan money from your IRA to an investor seeking rehab funds for properties he or she has purchased. You can loan money at a fixed interest rate or create an equity-participation note, where you share the profits when the property sells. In some markets, these returns can be dramatic. Additionally, you can secure the note with the real estate to be rehabbed, providing even more safety for your investment.

Purchasing an option to buy a property before a prescribed date for a fixed purchase price is another possibility. This involves locating a property that you believe is undervalued in the market. Later, if the terms of the option permit and the value of the property is greater than the optioned purchase price, the option can be resold—and all the proceeds and profits are returned to the IRA without tax ramifications. Some people like to buy tax liens at the county courthouse because they often provide a high level of safety. The liens may be removed and the interest paid in as little as 10 days or as long as six months. In rare instances, if the property taxes are not paid by the landowner, the tax lien holder (the IRA) could end up with title to the property.

Partnering with others is a great way for a small IRA holder to get a piece of a larger investment. This can be accomplished within an LLC, private stock, or simply with fractional ownership at titling. For example, an IRA can own an undivided 5 percent interest in an investment property and participate in all profits and expenses derived from the property at the 5 percent proportion.

Joel is a 26-year-old young professional. He worked his first three years out of college with a small community bank that offered him participation in a company-sponsored 401(k) plan. When he left his job with the bank, he rolled the vested 401(k) funds to a traditional IRA that offered self-direction so that he could have more control over his investments. Because he still has many years before retiring, he feels comfortable taking some risk and was intrigued by the prospect of speculating in real estate.

Since he only had $12,000 in his traditional IRA, he realized that he could not purchase a piece of property outright with such a small balance. He did some research and found that his IRA can partner with other parties to make a purchase. Several of Craig's friends decided to invest together in a piece of raw land not far from where they live. They ended up having five investors total: two IRAs and three individuals. All five are cash partners on the purchase. Craig submitted the appropriate paperwork to the IRA administrator, instructing him to initiate the purchase of 10 percent of the property with his IRA. On closing, all documents clearly specify each party involved and their respective percentage of ownership. Craig's IRA is responsible for 10 percent of all expenses of the property.

Two years later, property values nearly doubled, and the partners decided to sell. When the property sells, 10 percent of the proceeds will go back to Craig's IRA. At this point, he will not pay any capital gains tax on the appreciation because his share was held in the IRA. Craig now has nearly twice as much money to work with and is looking for his next opportunity.

Flexing Your Educational Dollars

Self-direction is not limited to retirement funds. You also can invest in accounts that operate like IRAs, but the funds can be used only for specific purposes, such as health and education.

Alfred and Lydia are in their early 30s and just had their first child. Soon after the birth, the proud grandparents suggested starting a college fund immediately, which they would be excited to contribute to. Alfred and Lydia began investigating different educational savings plans. They started looking at the traditional ways of investing, such as certificates of deposit (CDs), mutual funds, stocks, and bonds, but when Alfred analyzed the historical increases in college tuition and compared them with the growth of traditional investments, he was concerned. How were he and Lydia going to be able to meet the college expenses for their daughter while at the same time saving for their future retirement?

Lydia's older sister, Maggie, came to visit her niece on her first birthday and took the opportunity to brag about her new ventures as a realtor. When Alfred and Lydia spoke about their financial concerns, she had an answer for everything. She suggested that they open up a Coverdell educational savings account (ESA), which she explained could grow tax-free to pay for qualified education expenses. There is no limit to the number of ESAs that can be established for one beneficiary—so the grandparents could start one and so could Alfred and Lydia —and each participant could contribute up to $2,000 a year. On top of that, they could open a self-directed ESA and invest in real estate, which Maggie would be glad to help them with.

Alfred and Lydia laughed off the idea, not understanding how $2,000 a year in an ESA could afford real estate. But Maggie had a plan. She knew an area that had yet to be developed and thought that it had great potential. You could still find lots for around $15,000. Although there were only a couple of homes around these subdivisions, Maggie told them that the area could be booming in 18 years. Thus the two ESAs (Alfred and Lydia's and the grandparent's) could invest $4,000, and they could use their Roth IRAs to make up the difference. Each fund would own a prorated portion of the investment, and the only catch would be that they would all have to sell at the same time.

Although Lydia was skeptical at first, she saw the advantages. She thought it would be a stable investment unaffected by corporate scandal, and since it was a vacant lot, there wouldn't be any maintenance headaches or tenants to deal with. It was hard to admit that Maggie might be onto something, but it did address their future concerns. The more they looked into it, the more they realized that compared with their state's annual tuition increases, the real estate had outperformed the increase in the cost of earning a diploma.

Gliding toward Retirement

Nina is 50 and has money in various 401(k)s from different companies that she has worked for, which are invested in mutual funds and stocks. She has been a diligent saver, taking advantage of any matching programs that were offered. She also has contributed toward a Roth IRA every year that she could. She is considering diversifying into real estate because she feels that the financial markets aren't as secure as she would like them to be and aren't giving the return that she needs with the 20 years she has left to contribute to her retirement funds.

She had heard that she could invest her retirement funds in other types of assets if she found a custodian that offered self-direction. She asks around and discovers that there are several companies that offer self-directed custodial services. She begins by asking each of the companies a few questions. She's concerned that the custodian, administrators, and record keepers have a history of providing the kinds of services that she is looking for so that she can review their track record. She would prefer to find someone local but realizes that that doesn't have to be a top concern because much is done via telephone and mail. She checks whether any of them offer classes or instructional material to better understand what she is venturing into. She learns that such companies should not be offering investment advice or recommendations—that their role is just as a custodian and administrator. Then she compares fees for the services before making a final decision.

After she selects a custodian, she rolls over the funds in her 401(k)s into a fully self-directed IRA that allows her to invest in real estate, among other things. Nina wants to put her retirement dollars into rental property. She has bought and sold three homes over the years and feels comfortable with the process of researching a neighborhood, inspecting the property, and doing the paperwork involved. She decides to start with a single-family home in a neighborhood that is currently undervalued. She thinks that in a few years she could sell the home for a nice profit and invest in a multiunit building and, in the meantime, her IRA will be getting the rental income.

Buying a single-family rental property with funds in your IRA or qualified plan involves 10 basic steps:

1. Open a self-directed IRA or become a participant in a qualified plan that permits full self-direction.
2. Locate an investment property.
3. Make an offer on the property, generally in the name of the plan (e.g., purchaser: The Entrust Group, Inc., FBO Jay Jones IRA or Jay Jones Defined Contribution Plan).
4. If the offer is accepted, complete and submit a buy direction letter for real estate. The buy direction letter describes the purchase in detail and indicates where the administrator should send the earnest money deposit and/or option fee. You should include the purchase agreement or contract, which has been read and approved by you. Your administrator signs the contract on behalf of your IRA and forwards it to wherever you specify.
5. At closing, as with any real estate purchase, you read and approve all documents from the title company and/or escrow agent. These can include a settlement statement, warranty deed, title report, and others.
6. The title company and/or escrow agent sends the approved documents to your administrator, who signs them on behalf of your IRA or plan.

7. Rental or lease agreements are assigned by the seller to the plan. Any new rental or lease agreements then are made in the name of the plan. If you want to use external property management, property management agreements are signed between the plan and the property manager.

8. Your administrator sends the funds to the title company and/or escrow agent.

9. The deed is recorded in the name of your administrator for the benefit of your account (e.g., The Entrust Group, Inc., FBO Jay Jones IRA). The deed then is sent to your administrator.

10. All income is paid to your administrator for the benefit of your IRA or qualified plan. All expenses are paid from the IRA or plan in direct proportion of ownership.

So let's look at how Nina made this happen. The transaction unfolded as follows:

1. Nina opens her first self-directed IRA with Entrust using her 401(k) funds. Entrust is a third-party administrator that provides self-directed IRA services through a trustee bank. Nina's first real estate transaction involving her plan is the purchase of a single-family home.

2. Nina is familiar with the property and knows that the tenants have been there for over five years and aren't likely to move in the near future. The cash flow on the property is $12,000 per year gross and $9,600 net, which satisfies her plan's needs.

3. Nina decides to make an all-cash offer of $180,000. The current owner needs cash, so the timing is ideal. Nina makes an offer on the property in the name of the plan: The Entrust Group, Inc., FBO Nina Emmett IRA #123456789.

4. The seller accepts the offer. Nina completes a buy direction letter for real estate for the purchase of the property and sends it to Entrust, along with a copy of the contract that she had read and approved. Entrust signs the contract on behalf of her IRA and sends a $9,000 good-faith deposit to the title company from her IRA in accordance with the instructions in the buy direction letter.

5. A preliminary title report shows no prior liens or other conditions that would preclude the purchase. Nina reads and approves all the closing documents.

6. The title company, which is also her escrow agent, sends the approved documents to Entrust. Entrust signs them on behalf of Nina's IRA.

7. The rental agreement with the current tenants is assigned to the name of the IRA. Nina doesn't need a property manager because she just has one tenant, but she knows that if there is any work to be done, she shouldn't be doing it herself but rather have the IRA pay someone to do it.

8. Entrust sends the funds from Nina's IRA and the completed documents to the title company.

9. The deal closes. The deed is recorded in the name of Entrust for the benefit of Nina's IRA (The Entrust Group, Inc., FBO Nina Emmett IRA #123456789) and sent back to Entrust. Entrust maintains the deed in safekeeping. Nina's IRA now owns the property.

10. The tenants are instructed to make all payments to Entrust FBO Nina Emmett IRA #123456789. All income is deposited into an FDIC-insured cash account at the custodial bank. Service providers, such as utilities, insurance companies, and maintenance contractors, are instructed to bill the name of the IRA. All expense bills, including property taxes, are sent directly to Entrust to be paid from the IRA funds at the custodial bank.

As you can see, the purchase of a property in an IRA is as straightforward as making that purchase personally. The only difference is that there is an intermediary performing the transaction on behalf of the IRA.

Where's the Money? Comparing Options

When using retirement funds to invest in real estate, you want to consider the potential income and profit that you may derive, as well as the tax implications—now and in the future. Basically, if your investment accumulates income or profit that is tax-free, the growth rate is better than when your investment is taxed. If your accumulated investment or profit is tax-deferred and you must take distributions at your ordinary tax rate, the considerations may be different in terms of what you invest with (personal cash or retirement funds).

Doing the math is essential. There are four major alternatives to consider when investing in real estate:

- Using personal funds and taking advantage of tax write-offs
- Using tax-deferred retirement accounts, such as a traditional IRA
- Using tax-free retirement accounts, such as a Roth IRA
- Using tax-deferred exchanges, such as a 1031 exchange

Then, if you take these four alternatives and add the factor of debt financing, you have eight possibilities with different tax consequences.

Using the same dollar amount invested in the same property over 10 years, the results stack up like this: For an all-cash transaction, almost invariably, a Roth IRA is the best alternative in the long run, even beyond 10 years. In addition, you're not required to take distributions. The traditional IRA (and other tax-deferred options) have distribution requirements at age 70½, and depending on your income at that time, you could be taxed on the distribution. Otherwise, you do not pay tax while the investment grows. As far as taxes payable, 1031 exchanges and individual returns come in third and fourth, respectively. The individual return pays more than twice as much tax on an average transaction than a 1031 exchange.

When a real estate investment is purchased with borrowed funds (debt-financed), the results are very different and depend on the amount of debt financing involved. Depending on the type of retirement account you use, you could be subject to unrelated business income tax. This is discussed in-depth in Chapter 6.

For example, at a 70 percent loan-to-value (LTV) ratio using IRAs only, 1031 exchanges are the least taxed, followed by the IRAs. Personal invested dollars are taxed the most. Of the two IRA options, a Roth IRA comes out better because the distributions aren't taxed. However, if the loan has a 40 percent LTV ratio, both IRA options are better than a 1031 exchange. You also should take into account that a traditional IRA offers the advantage that contributions are made from pretax dollars, thereby lowering your current tax obligation.

Acquisition debt in a qualified plan is not subject to unrelated business tax income, so it is the best vehicle for investing in property that is debt-financed. However, distributions are required at age 70½, and they may be taxed depending on your income.

Table 1-1 is a spreadsheet that shows the four types of tax-advantaged transactions that can be used for investing in a rental property over a span of 10 years. It shows the amount of tax that would be owed when the property is sold. All the factors are the same except for the types of funds used.

Planning ahead is the most essential part of deciding which kind of tax-advantaged plan to use. Each option has different characteristics and qualification issues. Before we take a further look at the different types of transactions you can make, ranging from the simple to more complex, you should decide what kind of retirement account you want or have to work with, as discussed in Chapter 2. The real estate investments you choose may be influenced by the type of account you have and, of course, the amount of money in that account.

TABLE 1-1 Four Examples of Tax-Advantaged Transactions: Personal (One Inidvidual), Traditional IRA, Roth IRA, 1031 Exchange (Rental Income at $3,500 per Month)

No debt			Year 1	Year 2	Year 3	Year 4	Year 5	Year 6	Year 7	Year 8	Year 9	Year 10	Year 10 Sale
Rental income	5,000	60,000	60,000	60,000	60,000	60,000	60,000	60,000	60,000	60,000	60,000	60,000	60,000
RE tax & insurance	1,000,000	20,000	(20,000)	(20,000)	(20,000)	(20,000)	(20,000)	(20,000)	(20,000)	(20,000)	(20,000)	(20,000)	(20,000)
Depreciation	750,000	27,273	(27,273)	(27,273)	(27,273)	(27,273)	(27,273)	(27,273)	(27,273)	(27,273)	(27,273)	(27,273)	(27,273)
Mortgage interest			0	0	0	0	0	0	0	0	0	0	0
Rental Income (if not acquired from exchange)		12,727	12,727	12,727	12,727	12,727	12,727	12,727	12,727	12,727	12,727	12,727	0
Dissallowed depr (1031 exch)	(548,347)	19,940	19,940	19,940	19,940	19,940	19,940	19,940	19,940	19,940	19,940	19,940	
Rental income (if acquired via 1031 exch)		32,667	32,667	32,667	32,667	32,667	32,667	32,667	32,667	32,667			

		No Exchange	Prior Exchange
Sales price	1,500,000	1,500,000	1,500,000
Less purchase	(1,000,000)	(1,000,000)	(1,000,000)
Deferred gain	548,347	0	548,347
Addback acc depr	272,727	272,727	272,727
Adjust depr-exchange	(199,399)	0	(199,399)
Net capital gain	1,121,675	772,727	1,121,675

Ownership	Fed tax	Cap gain	Year 1 Tax	Year 2 Tax	Year 3 Tax	Year 4 Tax	Year 5 Tax	Year 6 Tax	Year 7 Tax	Year 8 Tax	Year 9 Tax	Year 10 Tax	Year 10 Sale Tax	Total Tax
Individual	35%	20%	4,455	4,455	4,455	4,455	4,455	4,455	4,455	4,455	4,455	4,455	154,545	**199,091**
IRA	35%	20%	0	0	0	0	0	0	0	0	0	0	0	**0**
Roth IRA	35%	20%	0	0	0	0	0	0	0	0	0	0	0	**0**
Individual & 1031	35%	20%	11,434	11,434	11,434	11,434	11,434	11,434	11,434	11,434	11,434	11,434	0	**114,335**

TABLE 1-1 Four Examples of Tax-Advantaged Transactions: Personal (One Individual), Traditional IRA, Roth IRA, 1031 Exchange (Rental Income at $3,500 per Month) *(continued)*

Debt financed		Year 1	Year 2	Year 3	Year 4	Year 5	Year 6	Year 7	Year 8	Year 9	Year 10	Year 10 Sale
Rental income	5,000	60,000	60,000	60,000	60,000	60,000	60,000	60,000	60,000	60,000	60,000	
RE tax & insurance	1,000,000	20,000	(20,000)	(20,000)	(20,000)	(20,000)	(20,000)	(20,000)	(20,000)	(20,000)	(20,000)	
Depreciation	750,000	27,273	(27,273)	(27,273)	(27,273)	(27,273)	(27,273)	(27,273)	(27,273)	(27,273)	(27,273)	
Mortgage interest	27,273	(48,133)	(46,155)	(44,033)	(41,758)	(39,319)	(36,703)	(33,898)	(30,891)	(27,666)	(24,208)	
700000 loan												
70% debt												
Rental income		**(35,406)**	**(33,428)**	**(31,306)**	**(29,031)**	**(26,592)**	**(23,976)**	**(21,171)**	**(18,164)**	**(14,939)**	**(11,481)**	
Unrelated business income	70%	(24,784)	(23,399)	(21,914)	(20,322)	(18,614)	(16,783)	(14,820)	(12,715)	(10,457)	(8,037)	
Rental income (if not acquired from 1031)		(35,406)	(33,428)	(31,306)	(29,031)	(26,592)	(23,976)	(21,171)	(18,164)	(14,939)	(11,481)	
Dissallowed depr (1031 exch)	(548,347.11)	19,940	19,940	19,940	19,940	19,940	19,940	19,940	19,940	19,940	19,940	
Rental income (if acquired from 1031)		**(15,466)**	**(13,488)**	**(11,366)**	**(9,091)**	**(6,652)**	**(4,036)**	**(1,231)**	**1,776**	**5,001**	**8,459**	
Unrelated business income	70%	(10,826)	(9,441)	(7,956)	(6,364)	(4,656)	(2,825)	(862)	1,243	3,501	5,921	

		No Exchange	Prior Exchange
Sales price	1,500,000	1,500,000	1,500,000
Less purchase	(1,000,000)	(1,000,000)	(1,000,000)
Deferred gain	548,347	0	548,347
Addback acc depr	272,727	272,727	272,727
Adjust depr-exchange	199,399	0	199,399
Net capital gain		772,727	1,520,473
Unrelated business income	70%	540,909	1,064,331

(continued on next page)

TABLE 1-1 Four Examples of Tax-Advantaged Transactions: Personal (One Inidvidual), Traditional IRA, Roth IRA, 1031 Exchange (Rental Income at $3,500 per Month) *(continued)*

Debt financed tax	Fed tax	Cap gain	Year 1 Tax	Year 2 Tax	Year 3 Tax	Year 4 Tax	Year 5 Tax	Year 6 Tax	Year 7 Tax	Year 8 Tax	Year 9 Tax	Year 10 Tax	Year 10 Sale Tax	Total
Ownership														
Individual	35%	20%	(12,392)	(11,700)	(10,957)	(10,161)	(9,307)	(8,392)	(7,410)	(6,357)	(5,229)	(4,018)	154,545	68,624
IRA	35%	20%	(8,674)	(8,190)	(7,670)	(7,113)	(6,515)	(5,874)	(5,187)	(4,450)	(3,660)	(2,813)	108,182	48,036
Roth IRA	35%	20%	(8,674)	(8,190)	(7,670)	(7,113)	(6,515)	(5,874)	(5,187)	(4,450)	(3,660)	(2,813)	108,182	48,036
Individual & 1031	35%	20%	(5,413)	(4,721)	(3,978)	(3,182)	(2,328)	(1,413)	(431)	622	1,750	2,961	0	(16,132)

Note: Capital gains rate is 20% (reduced to 15% for 2005–2008 tax years). IRA and Roth IRAs are not taxed unless they have unrelated business income (I.e., debt-financed income). IRA income is taxed on withdrawal. Roth IRA income is tax-free on withdrawal.

CHAPTER

Selecting a Self-Directed Retirement Plan

All retirement arrangements give you the opportunity to fund your future with profits from investments in a tax-free or tax-deferred environment. However, a self-directed retirement account lets you leverage your interest and knowledge in real estate and benefit from a variety of alternative investment opportunities. A fully self-directed retirement plan allows you to invest in any assets that are not prohibited by Treasury regulations and the Internal Revenue Service (IRS) Code.

The plan document you receive when you open your account provides specific information about the types of investments allowed, which can include some or all of the following investments:

- Accounts receivable financing
- Apartment buildings, co-ops, and condominiums
- Building bonds
- Commercial paper
- Commodities and futures accounts
- Contracts of sale

- Factoring
- Foreign sales corporation stock
- Gold bullion
- Improved or unimproved land (leveraged or unleveraged)
- Joint ventures
- Leases
- Like and unlike exchanges
- Limited-liability companies (LLCs)
- Limited partnerships
- Palladium
- Private placements
- Securities, certificates of deposits (CDs), stocks, bonds, and mutual funds
- Single-family and multiunit homes
- Tangible asset deeds
- Tax lien certificates
- Trust deeds and mortgage notes
- U.S. Treasury gold and silver coins

You can use individual retirement accounts (IRAs) or an employer-sponsored qualified plan such as a 401(k) to make the investments you want. This chapter provides an overview of the types of retirement plans you can set up either as an individual or as a self-employed person. If you already have a retirement plan that is not self-directed, you can transfer or roll over your current funds into a self-directed account.

IRAs

An IRA is a trust or custodial account for the exclusive benefit of you or your beneficiaries. IRAs are not qualified plans. Qualified plans are covered by the Employee Retirement Income Act (ERISA), whereas IRAs are not. The account is created by a written document, which must meet all the following requirements:

- The trustee or custodian must be a bank, a federally insured credit union, a savings and loan association, or an entity approved by the IRS to act as a trustee or custodian. (Any of these entities may hire other firms, such as third-party administrators, to perform the functions required on behalf of the trustee or custodian.)
- The trustee or custodian cannot accept contributions of more than the maximum allowable contribution for the current tax year. However, rollover contributions can be more.
- Your contributions must be in cash, unless it is a rollover contribution.
- The amount in your account must be fully vested at all times.
- Money in your account cannot be used to buy a life insurance policy.
- Assets in your account cannot be combined with other property, except in a common trust fund or common investment fund.
- You must start receiving distributions from your account according to the provisions of the type of IRA you have.

There are four types of IRAs: traditional, Roth, simplified employee pension (SEP), and SIMPLE. In addition, Coverdell education savings accounts and health savings accounts operate under similar rules as IRAs and also may be self-directed. If you are married, your spouse also can have either a traditional or Roth IRA, even if your spouse has no compensation.

To contribute to a traditional or Roth IRA, you or your spouse must have received taxable compensation during the year. Compensation includes wages, salaries, tips, professional fees, bonuses, commissions, and other amounts you receive for providing personal services. All taxable alimony and separate maintenance payments you receive under a decree of divorce or separate maintenance are treated as compensation.

If you are self-employed (a sole proprietor or a partner), compensation is your net earnings from your trade or business (provided that your personal services are material income-producing), reduced by your deduction for contributions on your behalf to other retirement plans and the deduction allowed for one-half of your self-employment tax. Compensation also includes earnings from self-employment that are not subject to self-employment tax because of your religious beliefs.

When you have both self-employment income and salaries and wages, your compensation is the sum of the amounts. If you have a net loss from self-employment, do not subtract the loss from salaries or wages you receive when figuring your total compensation.

Compensation does not include any of the following items:

- Earnings and profits from property, such as rental income, interest income, or dividend income
- Pension or annuity income
- Deferred compensation received (compensation payments postponed from a past year)
- Foreign earned income and housing cost amounts that you exclude from income
- Any other amounts that you exclude from income
- Income from an investment in a partnership if you do not provide services that are material income-producing

Quick Tips

- Always put funds in an IRA if you can. If you qualify, contribute to a Roth IRA. A Roth IRA generally is preferable because the gains are never taxed. If you do not qualify for a Roth IRA, a traditional IRA can be used. However, gains are taxed when you start taking distributions later.
- The amount you put away is not taxed in the year you make the contribution (unless it is contributed to a Roth IRA).
- If you convert a traditional IRA to a Roth IRA, pay the taxes due with funds outside your IRA, if you can. This leaves more money in the IRA. You must qualify for a traditional-to-Roth-IRA conversion.

- If you already have an IRA and wish to self-direct it, all you need to do is open a self-directed IRA and then transfer the assets in the old IRA to your new self-directed IRA.
- If you had a 401(k), TSA, 403(b), or government-sponsored 457 plan from any previous employers, you can roll these over to any traditional IRA or qualified plan if the plan allows it.
- The paperwork is easy, and the process goes very quickly. It takes only two to four weeks to fund the new account by transferring or rolling over monies from your previous IRA and/or qualified plan.

Traditional IRAs

Any individual under 70½ years old who has earned income can contribute to a traditional IRA. With a traditional IRA, contributions are tax deductible. Earnings grow tax-free, but all withdrawals are taxed as income. You can contribute to a traditional IRA in addition to another retirement plan; however, you might not be able to deduct all your contributions. You can set up and contribute to an IRA up to the due date of your income tax return for that year.

You can start taking distributions without penalty at age 59½ but are required to take distributions by April 1 of the year after you reach age 70½. Withdrawals are taxed at your rate at the time of distribution, so a traditional IRA may be a good choice if you expect your tax rate to be lower when you start taking withdrawals.

Roth IRAs

Roth IRAs are funded with posttax earnings. Contributions to a Roth IRA are not tax deductible, but gains accumulate tax-free. You can withdraw the funds after age 59½, but there are no minimum distribution requirements. The amount you can contribute is based on your modified adjusted gross income (AGI). To make the maximum allowable contribution, your AGI must be below the amount specified by the IRS in a given year. If your AGI is higher, the amount you can contribute is gradually reduced. You can contribute to a Roth IRA regardless of your age. You can have a Roth IRA and another retirement plan as long as you meet the compensation requirements. If you contribute to both a Roth IRA and a traditional IRA, the contribution limit for the Roth IRA must be reduced by all contributions for the year to all traditional IRAs.

You may prefer having a Roth IRA over a traditional IRA if you expect your tax rate at retirement to be the same or higher than your current tax rate because your withdrawals are not taxed.

SEP IRAs

A SEP IRA allows an employer to make contributions toward an employee's retirement without becoming involved in more complex arrangements. A SEP IRA is treated as a profit-sharing plan. The contributions are made to a separate traditional IRA for each participant. Participants may establish the IRA at the institution of their choice, and the SEP IRA can be self-directed.

For SEP IRAs, a self-employed individual is considered an employee as well as an employer. If you are self-employed, compensation is your net earnings from self-employment. The amount you can deduct for contributions on your behalf and your compensation are dependent on each other. Your deduction for contributions on your behalf is determined using the IRS Rate Table for the Self-Employed or the Rate Worksheet for the Self-Employed.

You can set up and contribute to a SEP IRA up to the due date of your income tax return for that year. Contributions must be in the form of money (i.e., cash, check, or money order). However, you might be able to transfer or roll over property from another retirement plan to your SEP IRA. You can contribute and deduct up to 25 percent of an employee's compensation (up to an established maximum amount) each year to each participant's SEP IRA. When determining the 25 percent limit, compensation is limited to $200,000, not including the employer's contribution to the SEP IRA. These contributions are funded by the employer. An employer does not have to make contributions every year.

You cannot have a Roth SEP IRA; however, you can convert contributions in a SEP IRA to a Roth IRA.

SIMPLE IRAs

A savings incentive match plan for employees of small employers (SIMPLE) is a retirement plan that small employers (including self-employed individuals) can set up for the benefit of their employees. The plan is a written salary-reduction arrangement in which the employee elects to defer his or her compensation by a specified percentage each pay period. The employer then contributes the deferrals, along with a matching amount, to a SIMPLE IRA or SIMPLE 401(k) on behalf of the employee. The employee's contributions are excluded from gross income and therefore are not taxed. The funds are taxed when withdrawn. An employee also can choose to stop making elective deferrals at any time during the year.

SIMPLEs must be maintained on a calendar-year basis. The employer's required contribution on behalf of the employee is stated as a percentage of the employee's compensation and cannot exceed the allowable limit for the given tax year. Compensation for an employee is the total amount of wages reported on Form W-2, including elective deferrals. For a self-employed individual, compensation is the net earnings from self-employment before subtracting any contributions made to a SIMPLE IRA. These contributions are deductible by the employer.

A SIMPLE IRA must be the only retirement plan to which the employer contributes. However, an employer who maintains a qualified plan for collective-bargaining employees can have a SIMPLE IRA for non-collectively bargained employees.

As of 2006, employees can make up to $10,000 of tax-deductible contributions per year.

Coverdell Educational Savings Accounts (ESAs)

A Coverdell ESA is a trust or custodial account that operates similar to a Roth IRA, but the funds must be used exclusively for paying education expenses for the beneficiary. For tax purposes, you must designate that the account is a Coverdell ESA when created, but you can have a self-directed account. Currently, the annual contribution limit is $2,000 per beneficiary until the child reaches age 18. No contributions can be made after that unless the beneficiary has special needs. You can open a Coverdell ESA for any family member who is eligible, including cousins, nieces, and nephews. The account can be transferred to any member of the family who is under the age of 30, including the beneficiary's spouse.

Contributions are not tax deductible, but earnings accumulate tax-free, and withdrawals are not taxed when used for qualified education expenses. You can use the funds for tuition for elementary and secondary schools as well as for college and university expenses.

Health Savings Accounts (HSAs)

An HSA is a tax-exempt trust or custodial account that must be used exclusively for paying health care needs for the beneficiary. These can include dental, vision, and over-the-counter medicines. To qualify, the beneficiary must be covered under a high-deductible plan during the time when the contributions are made to the HSA. You also cannot be claimed as a dependent on someone else's tax return or be enrolled in Medicare.

For an individual, the monthly contribution limit is the lesser of $\frac{1}{12}$ of 100 percent of your health plan's annual deductible or $2,650. The minimum annual deductible is $1,000. For families, the monthly contribution limit is $5,250, and the minimum is $2,000.

You can contribute to an HSA up to age 65, and contributions must be made in cash. HSAs can be self-directed. Any income derived in the HSA is not taxed, and if the earnings are used for qualified medical expenses, they never will be taxed.

Distributions for other than medical expenses taken prior to age 65 are taxed at your current tax rate plus a 10 percent penalty. After age 65, withdrawals can be taken for any reason and are not subject to the 10 percent penalty.

Qualified Plans

Qualified plans are retirement plans that are approved by the Treasury Department. Although it is not required that a retirement plan be approved, it is advisable to have the IRS determine whether the plan qualifies under IRS Code.

Only employers can open qualified plans, but all employees, including the employer, can participate in the plan. The employer is responsible for maintaining the plan. If you own your own business but do not have employees, you are still considered an employer. Qualified plans set up by a self-employed person are also referred to as Keogh or HR-10 plans.

There are two basic types of qualified plans: defined-benefit plans and defined-contribution plans. Contributions to a defined-benefit plan are based on a computation of what is needed to provide determinable benefits to each plan participant. Defined-benefit plans require an actuary to analyze and define these contributions annually. Each participant is provided with an individual account, and each participant is required to contribute regularly.

A defined-contribution plan is an employer-based plan that may or may not include employer contributions. The exception is a money purchase pension plan, which requires contributions based on set percentages established in the plan.

Profit-Sharing Plans

A profit-sharing plan is a defined-contribution plan. Contributions to profit-sharing plans are discretionary and can vary from year to year. Each employee receives the same contribution, unless the plan is designed to take advantage of permitted disparity rules. Contributions usually are based on business profits, but according to the IRS rules, they also can be based on compensation. The IRS sets the maximum allowable deductible contribution. The employer takes the deduction for this contribution. The employer's contribution to each employee's account is not considered taxable income to the employees for the contribution year.

A profit-sharing plan can include a cash or deferred arrangement (such as a 401(k) plan) under which the employer and eligible employees can elect to contribute part of their before-tax earnings to the plan rather than receive the pay in cash. This contribution, called an *elective deferral*, and any earnings it acquires remain tax-free until the funds are distributed by the plan. If the plan permits, the employer can make additional matching contributions on behalf of the employee.

An employee can defer up to 100 percent of compensation up to a set maximum. This deferral does not count as part of the computation of the employer's contribution of 25 percent. For example, an employee who is 50 years old and has W-2 wages of $50,000, makes a $12,000 deferral to a 401(k). That same person as the employer also can make a $12,500 contribution to a profit-sharing plan for a total of $24,500.

A plan generally is funded by employer contributions. However, employees participating in the plan can be permitted to make contributions.

If you are self-employed, you can make contributions for yourself only if you have net earnings (compensation) from self-employment in the trade or business for which the plan was established. If you have a net loss from self-employment, you cannot make contributions for yourself for the year, even if you can contribute for common-law employees based on their compensation. Your net earnings must be from your personal services, not from your investments, which does not include your deduction for one-half of self-employment tax and the deduction for contributions on behalf of yourself to the plan.

As an employer, you usually can deduct contributions, including those made for your own retirement. Contributions and earnings are not taxed until distribution.

To deduct contributions for a tax year, your plan must be set up (adopted) by the last day of that tax year (December 31 for calendar-year employers). You can make deductible contributions for a tax year up to the due date of your tax return (plus extensions) for that year.

To determine your deduction limits if you contribute to more than one plan, treat all your qualified defined-contribution plans as a single plan and all your qualified defined-benefit plans as a single plan. If you are contributing to a profit-sharing plan, you must reduce the 25 percent deduction limit by your deduction for contributions to a SEP IRA. The contribution deduction is similar to that of a SEP IRA.

You can always make a contribution to an IRA even if you have maximized your contribution to other plans. You also can contribute to a Coverdell ESA in addition to another IRA.

401(k) Plans

A 401(k) plan allows employees to defer income from their pay and contribute that amount to a separate account for their retirement benefit. The employee always owns 100 percent of the amount contributed from his or her pay. In other words, an employee is fully vested in his or her own contribution. Contributions to a 401(k) are tax deferred.

Employers may match employee contributions on a dollar or percentage basis. Vesting schedules for employer matching contributions permit the employee to own a certain percentage of the match over a period of time.

Employees may borrow 50 percent of their vested plan balance to a maximum of $50,000 to be repaid in substantially equal installments at least over five years. If the loan is secured by property, the property becomes collateral for the plan, and you may be entitled to a 30-year term to repay the debt. The interest rate must be at least the imputed interest rate as applicable to meet IRS guidelines.

Individual(k) Plans

An individual(k) plan is a self-directed profit-sharing plan with a 401(k) option for business owners with no employees. It is similar to a group 401(k) plan. Businesses that may use an individual(k) include corporations, partnerships, and sole proprietorships. An individual(k) does not fall under ERISA.

With an individual(k) plan, you are the trustee and administrator of your plan, which means that you can have checkbook control over the plan if you want. You also can hire a custodian or administrator to handle this if you prefer.

Other advantages are that the contribution levels are the highest for a person whose W-2 or Schedule C AGI is up to $160,000, and retirement is set at age 55, not 59½, so distributions can be taken earlier without penalty. In addition, in-kind contributions can be made; that is, you may contribute any asset you or your company owns that is not disallowed. The contribution must be made at fair market value, and all contribution limits still apply.

Qualified Roth Contribution (Roth 401(k))

Beginning in 2006, 401(k) contributions can be made on a posttax basis and placed into a tax-free account, similar to a Roth IRA. This Roth-like option has a special feature in that the usual restrictions of maximum income for an individual or married person are not in play. Thus, for those who haven't been able to contribute to a Roth in the past because of making too much money, now there is a new option. Because the Roth portion requires additional record-keeping, not every employer with a 401(k) plan will offer it because it drives the cost of administration up. Small plans and individual(k) plans are great candidates for the Roth 401(k). For real estate and other nonstandard investments where the return potential can be excellent, the higher deferral limits allow you to generate more tax-free income. Deferral limits for 2006 are $15,000. If you are 50 years of age or older, you can add another $5,000. Also, if you are eligible to contribute to a Roth IRA, you can make an additional contribution to your Roth IRA.

Like a regular Roth IRA, another big advantage of the Roth 401(k) is that the minimum distribution rules do not apply. Therefore, if you don't need the money for retirement, you can keep it growing tax-free in the account as long as you want, even after age 70½. You also may pass the account onto your beneficiaries tax-free.

Roth IRAs have been available since 1998, but because of the income limits, many taxpayers haven't been able to take advantage of them. For those who could contribute, the maximum contributions of $4,000 or less seemed puny compared with the maximum $42,000 contribution amounts available through company plans. With the new Roth 401(k), contributions are possible for all participants, regardless of gross income. Company matches and voluntary contributions to the 401(k) portion of the plan will remain tax deferred, as they are currently. There are no conversion provisions currently available to convert old 401(k) deferrals to Roth 401(k)s.

Individuals with small companies or who are self-employed and provide a SEP plan for their employees and themselves may wish to revisit the possibility of adopting a qualified plan with the Roth 401(k) option as a valuable alternative.

Table 2-1 presents a summary of maximum allowable contributions, and Table 2-2 provides a comparison of plan types for personal and business tax-deferred and tax-free investing.

TABLE 2-1   Summary of Maximum Allowable Contributions

	2006	2007	2008	2009
IRAs (Traditional and Roth)				
Up to age 50	$4,000	$4,000	$5,000	$5,000
Age 50+	$5,000	$5,000	$6,000	$6,000
401(K), 403(B), 457, and SAR-SEP plans				
Up to age 50	$15,000	$15,000*	$15,000*	$15,000*
Age 50+	$20,000	$20,000*	$20,000*	$20,000*
SIMPLE IRAs or SIMPLE 401(k)s				
Up to age 50	$10,000*	$10,000*	$10,000*	$10,000*
Age 50+	$12,500	$12,500*	$12,500*	$12,500*
SEP IRAs				
Self-employed individual or employer	Whichever is less: $443,000 or 25% of compensation for 2006. Deduction limit is 20%.			

*Indexed to inflation in $500 increments

TABLE 2-2   Comparing Plan Types for Personal and Business Tax-Deferred and Tax-Free Investing

Do you currently receive earned income (W-2 or Schedule C or F)?	No →	You are not currently eligible for an IRA or qualified plan.		
Yes ↓				
Are you self-employed?	No →	Does your employer offer a qualified plan, such as a Defined Benefit, 401(k), Profit Sharing or Money Purchase Plan, and/or a SEP?	No →	You are eligible to make fully deductible IRA contributions. If you eligible, those are contributions may be to Roth IRAs.
Yes ↓		Yes ↓		
		You may make IRA contributions. If you are eligible, those contributions may be to a Roth IRA. The deductibility depends on your earnings.		
Do you have a qualified plan, such as a Defined Benefit, Profit Sharing, or Money Purchase Pension Plan?	No →	You may establish a qualified plan, which includes a Defined Benefit Plan, Profit Sharing Plan and/or Money Purchase Plan. If you establish such a plan:	If you don't →	You may make IRA contributions. If you are eligible, those contributions may be to a Roth IRA. SEP and SIMPLE IRAs are other options you may have.

TABLE 2-2   Comparing Plan Types for Personal and Business Tax-Deferred and Tax-Free Investing *(continued)*

Yes ↓		Yes ↓		
You may make IRA contributions. If you are eligible, those contributions may be to a Roth IRA. The deductibility depends on your earnings.		You may make IRA contributions. If you are eligible, those contributions may be to a Roth IRA. The deductibility depends on your earnings.		
Do you have a SEP IRA or SIMPLE IRA?	No →	You may establish a SEP IRA.	No →	You may make IRA contributions. If you are eligible, those contributions may be to a Roth IRA.
Yes ↓		Yes ↓		
You may make IRA contributions in addition to your SEP or SIMPLE IRA contributions and, if you are eligible, those contributions may be to a Roth IRA. The deductibility depends on your earnings.		You may make IRA contributions in addition to your SEP contributions and, if you are eligible, those contributions may be to a Roth IRA. The deductibility depends on your earnings.		

What do you want in a tax-deferred plan?

	Profit Sharing/ 401(k)	SEP IRA	SIMPLE
As an employer, do you want to be able to contribute to your own IRA as an employee (up to 25% of unadjusted compensation for a given year)?	Yes To a maximum of $43,000.	Yes	To a maximum of $10,000.
As an employee, do you want to defer up to 100% of compensation?	Yes To a maximum of $15,000 plus catch-up provision. (Not counted as part of the 25% of your employer contribution)	Not available	To a maximum of $10,000 plus catch-up provision.
Do you want to self-direct all of your investments?	Yes	Yes	Yes

(continued on next page)

TABLE 2-2   Comparing Plan Types for Personal and Business Tax-Deferred and Tax-Free Investing *(continued)*

	Profit Sharing/ 401(k)	SEP IRA	SIMPLE
Do you want to be your own trustee, custodian and administrator? For example: Write and sign checks, sign all documents, and/or take possession of plan assets for your account.	Yes, or you may appoint others for each of these roles.	Not permitted	Not permitted
Do you want to borrow from your retirement account?	Yes, up to a maximum of $50,000 of your vested account balance.	Not permitted	Not permitted
Do you want to retire before age 59½ and receive distributions penalty free?	Yes, age 55 is an acceptable retirement age.	59½ is the earliest, without substantially equal periodic payments.	59½ is the earliest, without substantially equal periodic payments.
Do you want to make sure that your assets are protected from creditors?	Yes. Your benefits are not accessible to creditors, as ERISA provides for your benefits to be "non-alienable" providng your plan has common law employees.	No anti-alienation provision exists, but $1 million is exempt from bankruptcy (see Chapter 8, "Asset Protection").	No anti-alienation provision exists, but $1 million is exempt from bankruptcy (see Chapter 8, "Asset Protection").
Do you want life insurance as part of your retirement portfolio?	Yes	Prohibited	Prohibited
Do you want to be able to make in-kind contributions of assets that you own, not just cash?	Yes, provided that you have no common law employees, and the plan covers you, your spouse, and partners only.	Not permitted	Not permitted

Note: Percentages for self-employed individuals take into account the deductions allowed for one-half of the self-employment tax and contributions to the plan.

C H A P T E R

3

The Reicher Family Explores Its Contribution Limits

To understand how a family can use the various plans, let's look at the options available to Mitch Reicher, his wife Maureen, and his son Ezra. But first, here is their situation:

Mitch is 56, Maureen is 51, and their son Ezra just turned 17. Mitch and Maureen's modified adjusted gross income (AGI) for 2006 was exactly $100,000 and will be the same for 2007. This includes $80,000 in wages paid by Mitch's S corporation and the remaining profits from that company plus investment income. Maureen does not work outside the home, other than helping Mitch in his business. Mitch and Maureen file jointly on their taxes.

Ezra worked part time as a busboy at Old San Francisco Steakhouse in Houston in 2006 and earned $8,000. He expects to continue his employment there in 2007 and earn at least $10,000.

Mitch is a diligent saver and has plenty of cash to pay taxes on any Roth conversion he does, and his company also has plenty of cash in the bank. His family is covered by a high-deductible health plan (HDHP) with his maximum out-of-pocket expense of $5,450 for 2007 (it was $5,250 for 2006). This plan has been in place since January 1, 2005.

Maureen has $25,000 in a former employer's 401(k) plan, which she would like to use for investing in real estate and loans secured by real estate.

So here are their options for 2006:

Roth IRA. Since it is before April 17, 2007 (the contribution deadline for Roth IRAs for 2006) and Mitch and Maureen's modified AGI is less than $150,000, they can both still contribute for 2006 as well as for 2007. Even though Maureen does not earn wages, she still can contribute to a Roth IRA based on Mitch's income. Since Mitch is currently flush with cash, he decides to contribute $5,000 into each Roth for 2006 and $5,000 into each Roth for 2007. (They can each contribute the maximum, which is $4,000 a year plus a $1,000 catch-up for each year since they were both at least 50 years of age by December 31, 2006). Ezra also can contribute $4,000 to his own Roth IRA for 2006 and $4,000 for 2007, even if Mitch gives him the money to do so, because he had earned income exceeding $4,000 for 2006 and expects to do so again in 2007.

Traditional IRA. Maureen can roll her former employer's 401(k) plan into a traditional IRA. Maureen and Mitch instead could have contributed the amounts toward the Roth IRA into a traditional IRA or part of them as long as their total contributions didn't exceed $5,000 each per year. This would lower their current taxes because traditional IRAs use pretax dollars, but they elected to put their entire contribution into their Roth IRAs because they could afford to pay the taxes now and wanted to have the freedom of tax-free distributions without being limited to the mandatory minimum distribution requirements of a traditional IRA.

If Maureen wants to, she can convert the $25,000 from the traditional IRA into her Roth IRA in 2006 because their total modified AGI was $100,000 or less. Roth conversions are taxable in the year in which the funds are converted, but there is no penalty for doing a Roth conversion.

SEP IRA. Since Mitch is paid W-2 wages from his business, he can contribute up to 25 percent of his $80,000 wages into a SEP IRA, which is $24,000.

If he wants to, he also can begin making contributions for his 2007 SEP IRA. The money contributed to his SEP IRA comes from the employer, which in this case is Mitch's S corporation. If Mitch were self-employed and his Schedule C showed $80,000 net income from his business, he could contribute up to 20 percent of this amount, or $16,000 into his SEP IRA. The difference is that Mitch's corporation already has deducted the amount of the SEP IRA contribution and one-half the Social Security and Medicare taxes, whereas if he were self-employed, these amounts would get deducted on his personal tax return. This difference in contribution limits is intended to equalize the contributions based on the true net income after deducting half the Social Security and Medicare taxes and the contribution to the SEP IRA itself.

SIMPLE IRA. Another alternative is for Mitch to have a SIMPLE IRA at his company. This is not as advantageous at his income level but is appropriate if his income is less than $50,000 or if he has employees and doesn't want to contribute an equal percent into their retirement plans as he does for himself. SIMPLEs need to be established by October 1 of the tax year (in this case, October 1, 2006). With a SIMPLE, Mitch can defer $10,000 out of his salary, plus contribute $2,500 catch-up because he is 50. Additionally, Mitch's employer (his S corporation) adds another 3 percent of his salary, or $2,400. Thus the total is $14,900, which is less than Mitch can put into a SEP IRA.

Individual 401(k). The plan that Mitch can contribute the most to is an individual 401(k) plan. In this plan, Mitch can defer $15,000 plus a $5,000 catch-up for 2006 out of his $80,000 salary. In addition, Mitch's employer (his own S corporation) can contribute up to 25 percent of his wages into the plan, or $24,000. This means that Mitch can put $44,000 into his individual 401(k) plan! Starting in 2006, Mitch's salary deferral can be a Roth 401(k), which means that he pays taxes on his salary deferral when he contributes but will pay no taxes when the funds are distributed to him, provided they are qualified distributions. What an opportunity! Although Mitch qualifies for a Roth

IRA because of his income level, if he did make too much money to qualify for a Roth IRA, he could take advantage of the Roth 401(k), which has no income limits.

The three work plans, the SEP IRA, SIMPLE IRA, and 401(k), do not prevent Mitch and Maureen from contributing to a Roth or a traditional IRA but do affect the deductibility of a traditional IRA contribution.

Health savings account. Another way Maureen and Mitch can save taxes is to open a health savings account (HSA). To do this, they have to have an HDHP, which they've had since 2005. For 2006, they can contribute up to $5,450. Because Mitch is over 55 years of age, he can add a $700 catch-up for the year. Mitch and Maureen can split the contribution into two separate accounts or put all of it into one account. Contributions to HSAs are tax deductible, and there is no tax on the distributions if the money is used for qualified medical expenses.

Coverdell education savings account. Since Ezra is under age 18, Mitch can put up to $2,000 into a Coverdell ESA. Mitch receives no deduction for the contribution, but any earnings that are withdrawn for qualified education expenses are not taxed. Qualified education expenses include certain expenses for elementary school, high school, and college.

So here's what they decided to do for 2006.

TABLE 3-1   Maureen and Mitch's Plan for 2006

Family Member	Account Type	Amount
Mitch	Roth IRA	$5,000
Maureen	Roth IRA	$5,000
Ezra	Roth IRA	$4,000
Maureen	Rollover to a Traditional IRA	$25,000
Mitch	Individual 401k) Plan with a Roth option	$44,000
Family	HSA	$6,150
Ezra	CSA	$2,000
	Total	**$91,150**

Selecting a Custodian or Trustee for a Self-Directed IRA

For IRAs, the custodian or trustee is normally a bank, savings association, insurance company, or any other entity deemed by the Secretary of the Treasury to be able to carry out the responsibilities of a custodian or trustee of individual retirement arrangements. Custodians are regulated by a state and or federal agency. If the banks are depository banks, their deposits of cash are insured by the Federal Deposit Insurance Corporation (FDIC). If the trustees or custodians are nondepository banks, their regulator may require them to place uninvested cash deposits into FDIC-insured instruments.

From the point of view of safety, all custodians are equal. From the point of view of FDIC insurance, it is important to recognize that your uninvested cash is only insured in depository banks. The insurance only covers $130,000 in any single bank. If you deposit more than that, some banks spread your cash among several banks to take advantage of the $130,000 insurance limit per bank.

Banks are permitted to use record keepers of their choice. Some banks who act as custodians for self-directed IRAs and qualified plans appoint record keepers and administrators to provide the administrative and ministerial requirements of customers. In all cases, the bank who is shown as custodian is the legal custodian. The record keepers and administrators act as the agent for the custodian and provide you with the services that the custodian has contracted for.

The custodian, administrators, and record keepers should have a history of providing the kinds of services you are looking for so that you can review their track record. New entrants into the marketplace still may be developing that track record. It is important to find out if the staff of the custodian or administrator has specific knowledge about the investments you are about to make.

Because there can be absolutely no investment advice or recommendations, the custodian or administrator cannot give you any referrals to any source. Making a recommendation for an investment could violate that entity's regulatory underpinnings.

Location is an important consideration when doing transactions on behalf of your IRA or plan. Knowledge of local markets and what is required is very helpful to have your self-directed plan work smoothly and efficiently. If your custodian is local or has local record keepers and administrators, it is likely an excellent choice for you. You can visit their office and see for yourself how a self-directed operation really works.

Education is essential. Does your custodian offer classes to individuals, groups, or online? Are these classes certified? If your provider offers certified classes, you can be assured of a quality standard. Does the person with whom you work understand your transaction? Does the organization have the personnel that can accommodate your needs? How many professionals, such as attorneys, CPAs, and certified financial planners, are part of the team? Are they available to meet your needs? Getting answers to these questions will help you assess whether the provider is a good match.

There are several self-directed plan custodians in the United States. There are also offices throughout the United States that offer third-party record keeping and administration services, so you can find someone close to where you reside. The providers of comprehensive self-directed plan services include:

- The Entrust Group, with 30 offices throughout the United States
- Equity Trust, with one office in Ohio
- Fiserv, with two offices in Colorado
- International Bank and Trust, with one office in New Hampshire
- Sterling Trust, with one office in Texas owned by Matrix Bancorp
- Trustar, with one office in Delaware
- Pensco, with one office in New Hampshire (its holding company is in California)

Determining Whether the Account Is Self-Directed

The administrator, custodian, or trustee must provide you with an IRA custodial or trustee account disclosure and agreement. One article outlines the self-direction feature of the plan. The following example language is typical of completely self-directed plans:

> *Direction of Investment:* You have the exclusive responsibility for and control over the investment of the assets in your IRA. You shall direct all investment transactions, including earnings and proceeds from securities sales. Your selection of investments, however, shall be limited to publicly traded securities, mutual funds, money market instruments, and other investments that are *obtainable by us and that we are capable of holding* in the ordinary course of our business. In the absence of instructions from you, or if instructions are not in a form acceptable to us, we shall hold any uninvested amounts in cash, and we shall have no responsibility to invest uninvested cash unless and until directed by you. All transactions shall be subject to any and all applicable Federal and State laws and regulations and the rules, regulations, customs and usages of any exchange, market or clearing house where transactions are executed and to our policies and practices.

In the preceding paragraph, the phrase "obtainable by us and that we are capable of holding" means that the administrator can purchase the investment you selected on your behalf and that title to that investment can be perfected in the name of your trustee or custodian for your benefit.

Opening an Account

An IRA is a depository account from which you buy or sell assets. An account is created by a written document. Only an individual can establish an IRA. All of your assets are placed, or *vested*, in the name of the trustee or custodian for the benefit of your name and/or your account. The following information is required to open an account:

- All IRA applications require your personal name. This cannot be you and your spouse or the name of any trust. Only an individual can have an IRA.
- SEP IRAs require the employer name on the contribution agreement.
- The SEP agreement is separate from the IRA trust agreement in which the employer deposits the contributions made on your (the employee's) behalf (if the SEP is for the owner only, the same rules apply).
- You must supply your address and Social Security number. An Employer Identification Number is not required on the standard IRS Form 5305-SEP document because each participating individual must have an IRA.
- The type of account must be specified: IRA (regular or Roth) or SEP. You cannot have a SEP connected to a Roth IRA.

In addition to the required information, the following information might be requested:

- Beneficiary designation is not required at the time you open the account, but it is encouraged. Many custodians have merged the beneficiary designation with the application form, which includes a spousal consent form in community-property states. Beneficiary designation may be complicated and is subject to each individual case situation. It is always important to update beneficiary information as personal situations change.
- You may be asked to provide certain contribution and investment information on some forms. You only need to complete this if you make a contribution or transfer or roll over assets to your new account.
- Most providers ask that you sign an agreement with them. The agreement is not required by the IRS as a condition for opening an IRA, except that the provision for a backup withholding clause must be certified by you and generally is included in the application or agreement.

Selecting a Trustee for a Qualified Plan

If you are an employer or self-employed with no other employees, you may act as the trustee for your qualified plan. Unlike IRAs, there is no mandate to have a bank or other institution fulfill such a role, although they usually offer such services. You can select yourself, another individual or individuals, a corporation, or a combination as the trustee of your plan. Your choice of trustee depends on the type of plan, who the plan administrator is, what the scope of the plan is, and to what extent investment discretion is permitted.

Determining Whether the Plan Is Self-Directed

Setting up a qualified plan often involves filling out an adoption agreement associated with a plan document. The adoption agreement contains all the necessary information about the detailed functioning of the plan, and it determines how the plan operates in terms of eligibility, vesting, contributions, allocations, and so on. However, you can amend your plan in the future. The adoption agreement is part of the qualified retirement plan, which is the legal plan and trust under which your plan operates.

The investment section of the plan document provided by the plan sponsor outlines what you may invest in. The plan sponsor can be a bank, another financial institution, or an administrator. Typically, banks and brokerages limit investments to the products they sell. Most individually designed plans leave the investment section as flexible as possible. You should read all the information in the plan documents carefully to ensure that the plan meets your tax-deferred intent and flexibility in investment capabilities.

The following is a typical clause for complete self-direction:

If so indicated in the Adoption Agreement, each Participant may individually direct the Trustee (or Custodian, if applicable) regarding the investment of part or all of his or her Individual Account. To the extent so directed, the Employer, Plan Administrator, Trustee (or Custodian) and all other fiduciaries are relieved of their fiduciary responsibility under Section 404 of ERISA.

Setting Up a Plan

To set up a qualified plan, you can adopt an IRS-approved prototype or a master plan offered by a sponsoring organization, or you can prepare and adopt your own written plan that satisfies the qualification requirements of the IRS Code. (A sample adoption agreement is included in the Appendix.) The plan you establish must be in writing and be communicated to your employees. The plan's provisions must be stated in the plan—it is not sufficient merely to refer to a requirement of the IRS Code.

The plan must be for the exclusive benefit of employees or their beneficiaries, and you must allow them to participate in the plan if they meet the following minimum participation requirements:

- Are 21 years old
- Have been employed at least one year (two years if the plan provides that after two years of employment, employees have a nonforfeitable right to all their accrued benefit)

A plan cannot exclude an employee because he or she has reached a specified age.

Opening a Trust Account for a Qualified Plan

Unless your plan is funded completely with insurance, it must have a trust account for depositing contributions to the plan. The following items are needed to open a trust account:

- Your qualified retirement basic plan document
- Your adoption agreement
- The IRS opinion letter indicating approval for the plan

For the trust account, you must use the same taxpayer ID as the one used in your adoption agreement. You or another person or entity designated by you is the trustee, custodian, and administrator as indicated in your adoption agreement.

If your business is a corporation, a bank often will require a corporate resolution to do business with them. Usually, banks and other financial institutions, such as brokerages, supply the resolution.

Be careful that you do *not* open a qualified plan account with the financial institution. Let the institution know that you are opening a trust account for a retirement plan that you have established separately. To open a trust account, the financial institution should ask for copies of the preceding items. Often, the adoption agreement is sufficient. If the institution wants to make a copy of the basic plan document, it may do so.

The title of your trust account should say:

[*Your company name*] Profit Sharing Plan, for Benefit of [*your name*]

For example, "Alex Stewart, Inc., Profit Sharing Plan, FBO Alex Stewart" or "Alex Stewart, Inc., PS Plan, FBO Alex Stewart."

For tax purposes, it is important to have all vesting documents and titles use these terms. If you receive account statements or title and escrow information and they do not name the type of account in the title, for example, "profit sharing" or "PS," make sure that the financial institution corrects them immediately.

Once you have established an account, you can begin making contributions and investments.

As the plan administrator, you must keep records for all assets in your trust account. This includes every credit, debit, gain, and loss. If you have just one brokerage account handling all your investments, you can use the statements the company provides you. If you have multiple brokers and diverse assets, such as real property, notes, partnerships, and other investments, you should consolidate your records using a spreadsheet or accounting software.

Transferring Assets from Other Retirement Accounts

You can transfer funds to a self-directed IRA from any other IRA, and you can amend and restate your qualified plan to a self-directed plan.

Rollovers

A rollover is a distribution of cash or other assets from a retirement plan that is eligible to be put into another retirement plan. You can roll over a distribution tax-free, unless it is a return of an excess contribution or a required distribution. You can have the funds paid to you and then within 60 days deposit all or part into a new account, or you can transfer the funds directly to a different account.

If an eligible rollover distribution is paid to you, the payer must withhold 20 percent of it for federal tax withholding, so you actually are only receiving 80 percent of the distribution. This applies even if you plan to roll over the distribution to an IRA or another qualified plan. To avoid the 20 percent withholding, you can roll over the funds directly to an IRA or an eligible retirement plan. You can use any reasonable means to complete a direct rollover, including mailing a check, wiring the funds, or hand carrying the check to the receiving plan.

Rollovers are not tax deductible, but you must report the rollover distribution on your tax return. You must make the rollover within 60 days from when you received the distribution (the IRS can extend the time limit for certain hardship circumstances that are beyond your control). To defer taxes on the entire amount, you must roll over 100 percent of the distribution. You can roll over assets in kind, such as real property and notes.

If you withdraw assets from a plan, you can roll over part of the withdrawal tax-free into another retirement fund and keep the rest of it. The amount you keep generally is taxable (except for the part that is a return of nondeductible contributions) and might be subject to the 10 percent tax on premature distributions.

You can roll over assets from one IRA to another only once in a 12-month period. The time period begins on the date you received the distribution, not the date you rolled it over into another retirement plan. This once-a-year limit does not apply to employer-sponsored plans.

IRA distributions are exempt from the 12-month waiting period if the FDIC makes distributions as a receiver for a failed financial institution. However, you must roll over the same property you received from your old IRA into the new IRA. To qualify for the exception, the distribution must satisfy both the following requirements:

- It must not be initiated by either the custodial institution or the depositor.
- It must be made because the custodial institution is insolvent, and the receiver is unable to find a buyer for the institution.

Transferring from One IRA Trustee to Another

Transferring funds in your IRA from one trustee directly to another, either at your request or at the trustee's request, is not a rollover. Because there is no distribution to you, the transfer is tax-free. Because it is not a rollover, it is not affected by the 12-month waiting period that is required between rollovers from one IRA to another.

Transfers Because of Divorce

If an interest in an IRA or qualified plan is transferred from your spouse or former spouse to you by a divorce, separate maintenance decree, or a written document related to such a decree, such as a qualified domestic relations order (QDRO) in the case of qualified plans, the IRA or plan is treated as yours starting from the date of the transfer. The transfer is tax-free.

Timing of Funding

The most challenging part of opening a self-directed account is rolling over or transferring assets to the new account. A transfer can take days to months, depending on the assets and the capabilities of the institutions involved.

Cash can take up to 30 business days. You should allow at least 60 days to transfer assets other than cash. If you are rolling over from a qualified plan and the assets are deeds of trust, real estate, or privately held instruments, it might take months.

The plan document for a qualified plan usually states the time period required to complete a rollover or distribution, which can be up to 18 months from the date you terminated employment. From that point forward, reregistration and clerical issues can take additional time.

In the case of an annuity product in a qualified plan, insurance carriers operate on a completely different set of rules. Usually, they do not impose surrender charges on assets being rolled over to an IRA, but the time required to roll over may be lengthy.

In many cases, you can shorten the time of transfer by having assets distributed to you directly and then rolling them over in the 60-day time period mandated by law. This works particularly well with assets held as cash, stocks, bonds, or mutual funds. It is less effective with all other assets.

If you have a transaction that you wish to close quickly, liquidate the part of your portfolio that is easiest. Then transfer or roll over those assets to your self-directed plan or have them distributed to you and then roll them over to your self-directed plan.

Filing Transfer and Rollover Forms

The company you are transferring the funds to provides the appropriate forms for your transfer or rollover. Make sure that you provide the correct information.

In addition, you should check that the types of assets you are transferring or rolling over are accepted by the new custodian. This is generally not a problem for self-directed plans, except in the following cases:

- IRAs cannot accept life insurance policies from qualified plans.
- Some IRA custodians do not accept collectibles that were once legal, bullion, or debt-financed property.
- Some investment product providers do not transfer or roll over an investment that they do not offer, such as a certain type of annuity or a certain class of mutual fund, to a new plan.

When you are rolling over or transferring deeds of trust and real estate, the following might occur:

- Prior custodians or trustees do not provide the history of payments or other documents on a timely basis.
- Payers often make payments to the old trustee or servicer, and it can take time to correct such problems. Tax and assessor information is often incorrect for up to one or two years, and notices of default are not always received. Your current provider normally marshals the assets into your account, but the cooperation of the old provider is always important.

In many cases, signatures need to be medallion-guaranteed, which is an insured signature guarantee similar to a notary.

There are restrictions regarding minimum distribution requirements if you have taken a distribution or are in the year in which distributions must be taken.

The specifics usually are part of the transfer or rollover form. The restriction language includes information on the nature or method of calculations and beneficiaries. If this data is not included and you are in a minimum distribution year, your transfer might be rejected.

Converting a Traditional IRA to a Roth

Converting a traditional IRA to a Roth IRA is treated as a rollover. You can transfer contributions made to a traditional IRA into a Roth IRA without having to include them in your gross income if all the following apply:

- You transfer the contributions by the due date (not including extensions) for filing your tax return for the year you made the contributions to the traditional IRA.
- You transfer any earnings on the contributions.
- You did not claim a deduction for the contributions.

You cannot roll over amounts from a traditional IRA into a Roth IRA if your modified AGI for the year is more than $100,000 or if you are married and filing a separate return for the year. In addition, you cannot roll over required distributions from a traditional IRA.

You may convert property from a traditional IRA to a Roth IRA. The value of the property needs to be established as of the date you perform the conversion. You will receive a 1099-R from the traditional IRA (established by yourself or as a SEP IRA or SIMPLE) for the value of the property converted. For real property, fair market value that is established by a recent bona fide offer to purchase or an appraisal by a third party is acceptable, although in certain instances an assessor's valuation also might be permitted. For notes, fair market value is also acceptable. For private offerings, valuation needs to be substantiated through valuation or a recent purchase or sale.

For such valuations, you need to ensure that your documentation is clear and acceptable for examination by a third party, such as an IRS examiner.

Excess Contributions

If you contribute more to your plans than you can deduct for the year (nonde-ductible contributions), you can carry over and deduct the excess in later years. However, the carryover deduction, when combined with the deduction for the later year, cannot exceed the deduction limit for that year. Nondeductible contri-butions may be subject to a 10 percent excise tax.

C H A P T E R

Buying and Selling Real Estate

Handling real estate–related assets is more complex than handling standard assets such as stocks. A real estate transaction involves legal descriptions, price negotiations, title insurance, payment terms, and more. At first, this can seem overwhelming—as with any area involving financial and legal matters, the terminology and the paperwork required make it seem daunting. If you recall the first time you filled out a note or reviewed an escrow instruction form, it probably seemed hard to understand. The second time was easy.

The examples in this chapter show the variety of transactions you can make and creative ways that you can partner with your retirement funds. As with any investment, you should understand what is involved and feel comfortable with the choices you are making.

All-Cash Purchase Using IRA Funds

The simplest type of transaction is an all-cash purchase. In this way, you avoid finding lenders and paying tax on the profits of the debt-financed portion (see

Chapter 6). When making an all-cash purchase, a Roth account (either an individual retirement account (IRA) or a 401(k)) is the best alternative in the long run because you do not have to pay any tax on the profits. This usually holds true even when you take into account that you were taxed at the time you contributed the initial amount to the Roth compared with the opportunity of using the tax-deferred amounts of a traditional IRA. You are also not required to take a distribution at age 70½, as you would with a traditional IRA.

If your IRA (or qualified plan) is unable to pay for the entire purchase, you also can partner with someone else or yourself using either other retirement or personal funds, but first make sure that you are not entering into a prohibited transaction with disqualified persons, as described in Chapter 9. Partnering with someone has its risks in any venture, so be sure that you know and understand who you are working with.

Hundred Percent Down

Sid, who is 35 years old, has a 401(k) with his previous employer, Systron-Donner, where he had worked for 10 years. Sid's 401(k) contains $500,000, consisting of his contributions as well as his employer's. Instead of working for someone else, Sid has decided that he wants to start his own company, so he cashes in his stock from Systron-Donner, also worth $500,000. At the same time, he likes the prospect of investing in real estate in a rising market.

Sid has a tax accountant and certified financial planner who help him to explore having both his own business and investing in real estate. He begins by closing the 401(k) and rolling the funds into a self-directed IRA with EntrustUSA, which allows him to choose the types of investments, including real estate. Although the funds must first be rolled over into a traditional IRA, he requests that EntrustUSA immediately convert it to a Roth IRA so that his investments grow tax-free. Because Sid and his wife will make less than $100,000 in modified adjusted gross income (AGI) in the year, he can convert the funds to a Roth. He knows that he will have to pay tax on the amount converted and that the amount rolled over will be added to his income for the year. Because he had losses, the taxable amount is about 20 percent of the total amount, or $100,000. To start his new business, Sid does not need the full $500,000 that he received from the stock sale, so he uses $100,000 from that account to pay the taxes he owes.

Because Sid is 35, he has a long time before he will begin to use his retirement income, so his long-range plan is to maximize his tax-free investment portfolio. He also knows that if he ever needs to replenish his savings to run his fledgling business, he can withdraw up to $500,000 (his basis) from his Roth IRA without penalty or tax after five years. If he needs the funds earlier, he will have to pay a 10 percent penalty on the amount withdrawn.

Now that Sid has converted his retirement funds to a Roth IRA, he is ready to locate a property in which to invest. He determines that with the right property, he can rehab it and make a clear profit of nearly 40 percent in six months. He finds a property for $199,500, for which he makes an all-cash offer contingent on inspections. The offer is made in the name of Sid Brown, Roth IRA. Because Sid is a fiduciary to his own IRA and the IRA is to be the owner, Sid can sign the offer on behalf of his IRA.

Sid prepares a buy direction letter to direct EntrustUSA to purchase the property. The purchase contract is included with the buy direction letter. This letter also directs the administrator to wire transfer $5,000 to the title company as an earnest-money deposit. The administrator uses this direction letter to ensure that the transaction will be completed in accordance with Sid's instructions to EntrustUSA. Sid carefully reads and approves all documents involved in the purchase, but EntrustUSA signs all documents on behalf of Sid's IRA.

The property is inspected by an engineering and pest inspection firm to determine the condition. There are some plumbing and electrical problems and a pest infestation, amounting to approximately $7,500, so Sid negotiates with the seller to reduce the purchase price by $7,000. Sid amends his buy direction letter to $192,500 and faxes it to EntrustUSA.

There's a brief halt to the proceedings when Entrust notices that the buy direction letter does not match the preliminary title report. There had been a lot line adjustment at some point, which had been recorded, but the seller hadn't informed Sid. The seller wasn't aware that this was an important part of the transaction from Entrust's point of view, and it needed to be corrected to complete the purchase. Sid was glad that he had a third-party administrator that was paying attention.

After receiving the corrected buy direction letter, EntrustUSA wires $200,000 to escrow in accordance with the closing statement, which includes all closing costs and commissions. Hazard and flood insurance is obtained through Sid's insurance company; the insured party is the IRA. The deed, which reads "EntrustUSA, Sid Brown IRA," is sent to EntrustUSA for safekeeping.

Now Sid is ready to rehab the property. He knows that rehab costs need to be controlled to maximize his profit, so he reviews all bills and instructs EntrustUSA to pay them from his IRA. The bills are paid by EntrustUSA directly to the contractor. Sid acts as nominal manager of the project and does not receive any payment, and he does not employ any disqualified persons to work on the project, making this a sound and permitted investment.

Sid's Buy Direction Letter

The following information should be included in most real estate buy direction letters:

- The correct name and number of the account making the purchase because more than one account might be involved. For example, you might have a simplified employee pension (SEP) IRA and a Roth IRA to fund the purchase. In such cases, each plan receives a proportionate interest in the asset purchased.
- The property's address and location. This information is helpful in identifying the property and for documenting the purchase.
- The assessor's parcel number (APN) when available. In some jurisdictions, APNs are not used, so any other assessor identification could be used instead.
- The legal description of the property, especially if there is no APN. A legal description provides the most important source of identification for any real estate parcel.

- The names and contact information for the attorney, escrow agent, or title company handling the transaction.
- The total purchase price for the property. This is the amount you are paying to the seller for the property. It does not include any escrow fees, closing costs, or other adjustments that are assessed in the course of closing on the property.
- The amount that the trustee has advanced on your behalf. Sometimes this is referred to as an *earnest-money deposit.*
- The percentage of ownership for this account. The ownership interest is based on the proportionate amount of money coming from this particular account only. If you have funds from other accounts (your own and/or other account holders), a direction letter must be completed for each account involved in the transaction. For example, if you are funding 100 percent from your account, whether it is an entirely cash purchase or a down payment with a loan, the percentage of ownership for the account is 100 percent. If you are splitting the purchase in half between this account and someone else's, the percentage of ownership is 50 percent. If you personally and/or other disqualified persons are going to own a certain percentage, all the transactions must close at the same time.
- The names of the lender and property manager, when applicable, to clarify who is receiving the debt payments and who is collecting the rents that are forwarded to the account.

Howard and Jay Partner Their IRAs

Howard and Jay, who are friends but not "disqualified persons" as defined by the Internal Revenue Service (IRS) Code (see Chapter 9), have found an out-of-state rental property for $500,000 that they would like to buy with funds from their respective IRAs. The property has a lot going for it: a long-term tenant and a rent that has increased steadily over the years. And as an added bonus, Craig, the seller, is interested in managing the property after it changes hands. Howard and Jay each plan to contribute $250,000 from their IRAs, which will result in a 50/50 ownership arrangement.

The transaction takes 10 business days. Let's see how it's done.

Howard and Jay start by making their offer using the real property agreement, which lists their respective IRAs as the buyers, with each IRA purchasing an undivided interest in the property. A deposit of $4,000—$2,000 from each of their IRAs—is given to the title company. Since they don't want to take out a loan, the remaining amount of $496,000 will be wired to an escrow account at closing.

Immediately after providing the $4,000 deposit, each partner sends a buy direction letter to EntrustUSA, the administrator of both IRAs, instructing it to acquire the property on behalf of their IRAs. The buy direction letter includes information about the purchase, such as the property address, the assessor's parcel number, escrow and title company information, contacts for closing documents, purchase price, deposits, mortgage information (which in this case is none because there is no mortgage), percentage of ownership, and any other special instructions.

In the following days, EntrustUSA, relying on the instructions provided by the two buy direction letters, commences to complete the transaction on behalf of the partners' IRAs. EntrustUSA performs all the financial aspects, completes, reviews, signs the documents, and makes payments on behalf of the IRAs. Purchaser affidavits are obtained and notarized. The rental deposit made by the tenant (Dave) to the owner and now seller, Craig, becomes a settlement item on the settlement statement and is placed in a segregated account in each of their IRAs. Dave's rental agreement is endorsed to the partners' IRAs to ensure that postclosing rent payments are directed to those IRAs. By the end of the first week, they are ready to have a survey and pest inspection.

During the transaction's remaining three days, Howard and Jay review and approve all the relevant documents, after which EntrustUSA signs them on behalf of their respective IRAs. Howard's insurance company obtains hazard and flood insurance for the property, with Howard and Jay's IRAs as the insured parties. The homeowner's association is instructed to send all billings and notices to EntrustUSA.

At the closing, the title company records the deed and insures the title and then sends the deed to EntrustUSA for safekeeping. The vesting on the deed is "EntrustUSA FBO as to a 50 percent undivided interest, Jay Hall IRA and EntrustUSA FBO as to a 50 percent undivided interest, Howard Jones IRA."

Now that the 10-day transaction is completed, let's explore the future life of Howard and Jay's purchase. Tenant Dave's monthly rent payment of $2,500 is mailed directly to EntrustUSA, which, in turn, allocates $1,250 to each of Howard and Jay's IRAs, in keeping with their 50/50 ownership of the property. The monthly homeowner's association dues of $76 are paid from the IRAs by EntrustUSA, again at 50 percent each (or $38), as well as any other expenses, such as Craig's management fee. Likewise, the administrator pays the real property tax in equal proportion, in this case $1,350 per installment per IRA. Dave takes care of his own utilities in accordance with the rental agreement terms.

Both IRA administrator EntrustUSA and partners Howard and Jay have tax-reporting requirements with regard to the property. Every May, EntrustUSA files IRS Form 5498, IRA Contribution Information, which reports the fair market value of the property as of December 31 of the previous year. The fair market value represents the last fair market valuation that the IRA administrator received for the property. In this case, that value was determined by the bona fide offer to sell and the subsequent purchase price of $500,000. Howard and Jay each receive a Form 5498 from the administrator indicating the value of their IRAs at EntrustUSA and showing any and all IRA contributions made during the relevant tax year.

Howard and Jay must report their nondeductible contributions on IRS Form 8606, Nondeductible IRAs, which they will include with their tax returns. Because they didn't take any distributions from their IRAs, no distributions are reported to them by EntrustUSA on IRS Form 1099-R.

Howard and Jay's IRAs each now earn an average of $1000 a month and hold an asset that most likely will stay the same or increase in value over time. Also, by combining their resources, they were able to purchase the property without borrowing money, thereby avoiding paying taxes on debt-financed property.

Authorizing Periodic Payments

If periodic payments, such as mortgage payments, property taxes, management fees, or homeowner's association dues, need to be made from the account, you can set up payments with the administrator or trustee using a periodic payment authorization letter. A typical periodic payment authorization letter includes the following:

- Name and number of the account making the payments because more than one account may be involved.
- Address and location of the property for which payments are being made.
- Percentage of ownership held by this account, which is used to determine the proportionate amount of money to pay. Each account involved must have its own completed authorization letter.
- Type of payments to be made.

Investing in a Future Retirement Home

For over 15 years, the Hunter family vacationed in a beachside community, each time staying in the same condominium complex, renting from various owners. While their children were hanging out on the beach, they would grab the local real estate guide, noticing the condo prices going up each year. They fantasized about buying something for their retirement, but they didn't have enough savings to purchase one of the condos. One day they discovered that there were a few vacant lots available nearby, so they looked into purchasing raw land as an investment with their self-directed IRA.

They worked with a local realtor to select a vacant lot, and then they directed their IRA administrator to purchase the property in the name of their IRA. Once the $100,000 transaction was completed, the IRA was responsible for all taxes and homeowner's association fees.

They were happy with their IRA investment, but then Mark remembered that IRA investments must be passive—that the IRA beneficiary cannot gain any use from the property. The rub was that Mark's wife, Helen, had a dream of retiring to this seaside community, building on the IRA-owned land, and living the good life. Mark reminded her that the dream likely would be very expensive if they used the IRA-owned property because they would have to take a taxable distribution on the property first at the appraised price at the time of the distribution (e.g., assuming that the property would double in the intervening years before retirement, the tax rate would be ordinary income of $200,000).

After listening to Helen's pleas, Mark contacted his CPA to see if there was any way to transition the property from the IRA to personal use and avoid the future $200,000 tax liability for distribution. After studying their earnings and personal finances, their CPA suggested that Mark convert his traditional IRA to a Roth this year. Mark qualified for the conversion because his AGI for the year for him and his wife was less than $100,000. At first, Mark didn't understand how this could help. His CPA explained to him how Helen's dream of building and living on the land could be realized if it was owned in a Roth IRA. First, the appreciation of the land would continue to grow as it would in a traditional IRA. However, once Mark had a funded Roth account for five years and had reached the age of 59½ years, he could take a distribution from his Roth IRA without tax consequences. In this case, it would be the land. After taking the distribution, the Hunter's would have full use of the land for any lawful purpose, including building a retirement home.

So Mark converted his traditional IRA, and for that year his income was increased on his tax return by $100,000. (The property was converted to a Roth IRA soon after purchase; otherwise, an appraisal would have been required prior to conversion.) Mark paid the resulting taxes by April 15 of the year following the conversion. If he had not converted to a Roth IRA, Mark would have faced large tax consequences at the very time he and Helen would need the personal resources to build their retirement home. Thus, although they had some tax consequences the year they purchased the land, they knew that when they were ready to take a distribution, it was theirs, free and clear.

For more information on taking distributions, see Chapter 10.

Purchasing Fixers

Purchasing "fixer properties" or rehabs with retirement funds is a popular practice. There are three keys to success: (1) find a property that has the potential to realize a healthy profit after modifications are complete—in other words, know the market you're in; (2) make sure that your plan or IRA has adequate funds to finish the entire rehab—running out of funds in the middle of the job is a recipe for a loss; and (3) don't forget that you also need funds to take you through the postrehab, presale period.

Roberto Does Rehabs

Roberto is a flooring specialist who knows a lot about rehabbing properties. Confident in his skills and experience, he decides to oversee a project that will be owned by his account in his flooring company's 401(k) plan, which is a self-directed plan. Under a self-directed plan, employees can determine the types of investments made. (Owners are also considered employees under a self-directed qualified plan.)

Roberto commences the search and soon locates a "for sale by owner" property for $239,000. Based on recent comparable prices for good-quality homes in the same neighborhood, he believes that after a rehab, he can resell the property through a realtor for $349,000. His goal is keep the rehab expenses to 10 percent of the purchase price (about $25,000), and he estimates that realtor fees and closing costs will be another $25,000, totaling $50,000. This leaves him $50,000 from the sale, which adds up to a 20 percent profit in the three months he expects to rehab and sell the property.

Let's follow Roberto every step of the way:

Step 1: Roberto submits an offer of $240,000 for the property using a real property purchase agreement, which indicates that his 401(k) plan account is the buyer. The plan wires an earnest-money deposit of $5,000 to the escrow account established at a local title company.

Roberto wants to be sure that the property is worth what he expects and that his rehab costs will be in line with his projections. To that end, the purchase agreement has significant contingencies for inspections and for remedial action on the part of the seller.

Step 2: Roberto completes and sends the buy direction letter to the custodian of his flooring company plan, IB&T. Along with the description of the property and financial information, the buy direction letter lists his special instructions.

IB&T employs the services of a third-party record keeper (TPR) to perform the tasks in Roberto's buy direction letter. The transaction appears to be straightforward because it's closing with all cash.

Step 3: Determining the true condition of the property is critical for Roberto. He instructs the TPR to hire an inspector, who is also an engineer, to inspect the property thoroughly. The TPR also hires a pest control company of Roberto's choosing to examine potential issues regarding pests, radon, mold, and other related issues. His plan pays for the inspections, which is permissible.

Once the inspections are concluded to Roberto's satisfaction, the transaction closes within 30 days as agreed on with the seller. The deed to the property is vested as "Roberto Flooring Profit Sharing Plan, FBO Roberto Alvares, IB&T custodian." The deed is recorded, and the title is insured by the title company. The deed is sent to custodian IB&T for safekeeping.

Step 4: Roberto has made the purchase he wanted, at the price he wanted, with a prospect to turn a good profit on resale. The crucial second stage is to develop a budget for the rehab and determine that his plan has sufficient funds to support that budget.

Relying on an expanded checklist of the original inspection worksheet that was used to evaluate the property's condition prior to sale, Roberto produces an estimate range of $37,800 to $48,800. Hiring a general contractor would push costs above Roberto's high-end estimate, so he takes on that role himself. Since he can't do the rehab work, he directs his plan to hire the subcontractors. In addition, he establishes a reserve fund for contingencies such as unexpected expenses.

Step 5: Within 90 days, the rehab is complete. Table 4-1 shows Roberto's estimated budget figures compared with his actual expenditures.

TABLE 4-1   Roberto's Estimated Budget versus Actual Expenditures

Item	Estimate		Supplier	Actual	Change	Change
	From	To			From Low	From High
Windows/doors	$ 1,000	$ 1,000	A and S Lumber	$ 900	$ 100	$ (100)
Plumbing/ME	1,500	2,000	Franz Plumbing	2,000	(500)	0
Electrical/lighting	2,000	3,000	SJ Lighting/Electrical	3,100	(1,100)	100
Sheetrock	2,000	3,000	Curtis Drywall	2,000	0	(1,000)
Painting	1,000	2,000	Salvador Floor & Paint	1,800	(800)	(200)
Cabinetry	3,000	4,000	Premier Kitchens	3,000	0	(1,000)
Finish carpentry	2,000	3,000	Premier Kitchens	3,000	(1,000)	0
Stone counters	2,500	3,000	Instone Design Works	3,500	(1,000)	500
Tile	1,500	2,000	Instone Design Works	1,500	0	(500)
Hardwood	2,500	3,000	Salvador Flooring	1,800	700	(1,200)
Carpets	1,000	1,500	County Floor Coverings	1,300	(300)	(200)
Bathroom	3,000	4,000	Jack's Bathrooms	3,500	(500)	(500)
Appliances	3,000	3,500	Fred's Appliances	3,500	(500)	0
Closets	1,500	3,000	Closet Builders	2,000	(500)	(1,000)
HVAC	4,000	5,000	Downing HVAC	4,000	0	(1,000)
Pest/radon	1,000	1,000	R and D Pest Control	1,000	0	0
Contingency	5,000	5,000		0	5,000	(5,000)
Permits	800	800		800	0	0
	$38,300	$49,800		$38,700	$ (400)	$(11,100)

As we can see, the rehab project comes in a mere $400 above Roberto's low budget estimate and more than $10,000 below his high budget estimate. But let's look more closely at a potentially costly issue that arose during the rehab. During drywall work, the subcontractor discovered a persistent leak behind the kitchen wall that appeared to be coming from the roof. It was possible that as much as $12,000 would be needed for the repair, pushing the overall total near $50,000 and thus above the high budget estimate.

Before the first day of work had begun, Roberto had prepared for just such a problem. He negotiated with a lender to provide his plan with up to $50,000 in nonrecourse financing if necessary. The borrower would be the plan, and the collateral would be the property. The plan's TPR was permitted under the contract with custodian IB&T to sign on behalf of Roberto's plan account as the borrower. Roberto was not permitted to sign as the borrower, nor could he use his credit to obtain the loan. He had other assets in his plan that he could have used as a worst-case contingency reserve, but he chose not to do so.

Fortunately, the water leak was traced to an improperly installed vent pipe, and the cost of repair was minimal, which kept the rehab total near Roberto's low budget estimate. But had it proved more costly, Roberto would have been able to meet the need because he had planned for possible contingencies through adequate debt financing.

Step 7: With the rehab finished, it's time for Roberto to make the sale. He reviews his costs to date: $250,000 to purchase the property, including closing costs and transfer taxes, and $38,700 for the rehab, which brings his plan's investment thus far to $288,700. He sets an asking price of $379,000, expecting an actual sale of $349,000. His initial gross profit would be $60,300, or 21 percent over the original purchase price plus renovation costs.

Of course, selling the property will incur additional costs. The costs associated with closing and commissions could reduce the net to his plan to $34,360, representing a gross profit of 12 percent, far from the 20 percent he wanted initially. Because Roberto wants his plan to maximize its profit potential, he calculates that if the plan, rather than an agent, sells the property, the profit could climb to $44,830, or 15.5 percent (assuming a 3 percent commission), or as high as $55,300, or 19 percent (no commission). Closing costs of $5,000 would be the same, regardless of who sold it.

Roberto's decision to sell directly is rewarded in this case: His plan sold to a realtor! The plan, after closing costs and including the 3 percent commission, realizes $44,830—not too far from his original goal of a $50,000 profit.

Step 8: The sale of the property is consummated between Roberto's plan and the buyer. A purchase contract is drawn up by the buyer, and Roberto completes sell instructions for the TPR to follow. The contract is signed by the TPR on behalf of Roberto's plan.

Positive Cash Flow and Appreciation

Real estate has a history of appreciating, and depending on the type of investment, it also can provide an added income stream for your retirement fund. Many people who invest in rental or commercial property choose to hire a property manager to handle the day-to-day operations. By doing this, you don't have to worry about the issue of providing services to your plan and just how much is too much in terms of prohibited transactions. If your IRA is partnering with others in the investment, having a property manager is also a way to deal with rent checks that otherwise would need to be made payable to each partner individually. With a manager or management firm, tenants write their checks to one entity. The manager handles all the rent collection and payment of bills. Having a manager also means that you won't have to deal with tenant emergencies, which almost always seem to occur in the middle of the night. This service does have a cost, however, and some investors choose to go it alone to save on those costs.

Unfortunately, there are no specifics in the Internal Revenue Service (IRS) regulations that address exactly how much service the owner of an individual retirement account (IRA) can provide to the plan or property held within it. If your plan is holding a one- or two-family property and once a year you advertise and show the apartment to find a new tenant, this should be an activity that is allowed. However, if you are holding a 50-unit property and have frequent turnovers or a vacation property that rents by the week, it's advisable to not handle the rentals yourself. The same is true for any maintenance or repairs to a property. If a tenant calls with a plumbing emergency and you respond to clear a pipe, this should be an allowable activity. Renovating a kitchen or bathroom on your own would not be allowed. The manager cannot be a disqualified person, which includes yourself, your spouse, and any ascendants or descendants and their spouses. Nor can any firm retained to manage the property be controlled by a disqualified person. The same holds true for any contractor or firm retained for repairs.

Chuck Buys a House Instead of CDs

Positive cash flow and appreciation are admirable goals, and often they go hand in hand for an investor. Chuck, who has all his savings in an IRA as cash, is considering investing some of the money in Florida real estate but, of course, he wants his rental property to have a positive cash flow. The bar he sets for his investment is a 7 percent return—2 percent to cover inflation and 5 percent net profit.

Chuck takes the plunge, using $244,000 from his IRA funds to purchase a $229,000 property with $15,000 in closing costs. So what does he need to reach his target investment return of 7 percent? He projects a rental income of $1,950 a month. After he subtracts $300 for real estate taxes plus insurance and $195 for property management fees, the monthly income drops to $1,455, or a 5.9 percent return. However, if Chuck foregoes a property manager, the return climbs to 7.1 percent, and he clears the bar.

All is well and good until it turns out that Chuck can get a monthly rent of only $1,450. Even without a property manager's services, his rate of return falls to 5.36 percent. On the other hand, though, the investment return to his IRA is tax-free, and the appreciation of property values in that area of Florida has been about 16 percent annually. Still, he doubts that such a strong rate of appreciation will last forever.

Chuck ponders his overall strategy. If he sells the property after one year, the 16 percent appreciation will net his IRA close to $13,500, for a return of about 4.8 percent (after factoring in a 5 percent commission and 4 percent for closing and transfer costs). Therefore, selling after one year is a no-go, unless he thinks he can reinvest in another rental property for a significantly better return. Then again, a new sale means more commissions and closing costs, so the appreciation and rents would have to be really good to make it worth his while.

If Chuck holds onto the property, he is reasonably sure that the rent will go up over time. The property is under a one-year rental agreement, and based on trends in the area, he believes that he'll be able to raise the rent by $100 a month each year, producing at least a 5.7 percent annualized return on the original investment. Additionally, he will place the net income from the rental property in a 2.5 percent FDIC-insured money market account. Calculated over a 20-year period, even without adding rent increases or other changes in income, the account's yield would approach $75,000.

Thus, although Chuck won't get the 7 percent investment return he had set at the beginning, he isn't entirely disappointed. He could have gone with certificates of deposit (CDs) at a 5.25 percent yield over 20 years that paid semiannually, but such instruments lack flexibility. He is confident that his real estate property will appreciate over time and that his income from the property will equal, if not exceed, the yield from a CD. He concludes that his Florida property is a sound investment.

Developing Their Retirement Funds

Michelle and Charles are real estate investors and have done transactions together for many years on an undivided-interest basis. They funded condominium conversions where they took actual units as their profit interests. They purchased land, subdivided the property, and sold lots. They accomplished these and other such transactions by using investments from their Keogh plans (tax-deferred plans for self-employed individuals that work like other qualified retirement plans).

Having made handsome profits over the years, Michelle and Charles's plan accounts climbed above $3 million each. In 1999, when they both chose to semi-retire and their earned income dropped to zero, they decided to convert large portions of their respective qualified plans to traditional IRAs and then convert those funds to Roth IRAs. Their goal was to live off income from their Roth IRAs when they turned 59½ because at that age they would not incur any penalties from those tax-free distributions.

To bring them closer to their desired goal, Michelle and Charles became involved in purchasing a single property to be developed as a strip mall. They began by each converting $1 million in qualified plan money to Roth IRAs and immediately paying their respective tax of almost $250,000 from personal funds. Their Keogh plans had in-service withdrawal provisions that allowed for the withdrawal and subsequent rollover to an IRA.

Bruce, an experienced developer they knew well, found a perfect property that would come in slightly under $2 million after acquiring the land and developing it, as well as factoring in architect's fees, contractors' fees, and of course, Bruce's fee. The resulting income on the property was estimated to have a capitalization rate of 7.75 percent. Michelle and Charles agreed that the property looked promising for a strip mall and decided to invest in the land and its subsequent development with their Roth IRAs. Each IRA would own a 50 percent interest in the property, which included an equal undivided interest in the development. Because Michelle, Charles, and Bruce were unrelated persons and did not own any part of a business together, they were in little danger of conducting a prohibited transaction.

The following steps were involved in the transaction:

Purchasing the land. To acquire the land, which was priced at $500,000, EntrustUSA executed a purchase contract on behalf of the Roth IRAs as undivided interest—50 percent each. The contract was accompanied by buy direction letters from Michelle and Charles.

Contracting for development. The Roth IRAs contracted with Bruce to build the property for $1.5 million, with these funds divided equally between the two Roths. The contract stipulated 120 days for completion of the project after permits were obtained.

Obtaining the standby letter of credit. The $1.5 million buildout also was guaranteed by a standby letter of credit to the Roth IRAs from a private lender. This allowed for the $1.5 million to be used for other investment purposes during the permit process. The debt financing would occur only if cash funds were unavailable once the permits had been obtained, at which point the creditor would encumber the property held by the Roth IRAs. If cash was available, the debt financing would not be required. Because the Roth IRAs paid a fee to obtain the standby letter of credit, the transaction was considered to be debt financed.

Since Michelle and Charles had no interest in selling the property immediately on completion, the debt-financing component was not a problem. They were confident that their Roth funds would not fall short once the permit process was complete. Even if their Roths needed to draw on the letter of credit, Michelle and Charles believed that they would have cleared out any debt-financed property obligations because unrelated debt-financed income tax does not apply if the asset is out of debt for the 12-month period before the sale.

Completing the project. The permit process for the strip mall took almost six months. Bruce then had another 120 days to complete the project, as per his contract with the Roth IRAs. Meanwhile, the land owned by the Roths continued to appreciate, with values climbing about 11 percent that year. Bruce lined up an anchor tenant, a national-brand retail clothier who liked boutique locations. By the time the project was completed, the strip mall was completely leased.

During the development, Bruce had Michelle and Charles approve "draws" from their respective Roth IRAs using the standard builder control five-draw system, which provided for the release of funds to coincide with various stages of construction. EntrustUSA, acting as the builder control for the draws, was paid an additional fee from the Roth IRAs. Although the standby letter of credit was never used, the Roth IRAs still paid the related fee of ⅛ percent.

Bruce handled all subsequent income and expenses for the strip mall and sent the net checks to EntrustUSA to be credited to Michelle and Charles's respective Roth IRAs.

Selling the property. A couple of years later, Bruce decided that he wanted to own the mall himself because it fit nicely into his long-term financial plans. Because he had provided services under contract to the Roth IRAs of Michelle and Charles, he considered himself a "disqualified person" and therefore could not make the purchase. However, a clause in his initial agreement with the IRAs allowed him to act as a broker for the sale of the property and to charge a fee for such services.

A fellow developer, Paula, who was not a disqualified person, liked the property and made a $4.75 million offer to the Roth IRAs. Accepting the offer, Michelle and Charles each prepared a sell direction letter and sent them to EntrustUSA.

Handling the postsale income. After the sale was concluded to Paula, the Roth IRAs, which each started with $1 million, ended up more than doubling in income. This worked out to an annual return of slightly more than 25 percent, never to be taxed again. Adjusting for taxes paid and an income of 9 percent on the amount of tax on $500,000 for three years, the return was closer to 18 percent per year.

Reinvesting the income. Michelle and Charles had always intended reinvestment to be a part of their strategy. After the sale of the strip mall to Paula, they directed their respective Roth IRAs to become lenders to Bruce for his other development projects. They each prepared a buy direction letter for notes in the form of a letter of credit that Bruce could draw on regularly. Bruce, in turn, paid them 12 percent annually on notes secured by first position on real property that he was developing. It was cheap money for Bruce from a reliable source and terrific tax-free income for Michelle and Charles from their Roth IRAs.

Taking distributions. When Michelle and Charles reached age 59½, they each began receiving distributions from their Roth IRAs. They prepared distribution requests and sent them to EntrustUSA for execution. EntrustUSA sent them the requested funds and a 1099-R with a reason code of Q (indicating a qualified Roth IRA distribution).

Options

An option agreement provides for the purchase of property at a predetermined price within a specified time period. The agreement spells out the terms and conditions of the purchase, as well as the consideration. The consideration is usually cash or property that is acceptable to the parties who are to be paid by the investor. If the investor does not exercise the option during the specified period, the option expires, and the consideration usually is forfeited to the seller. In the case of IRAs and qualified plans, the investor is the IRA or qualified plan.

During the period of the option, the investor has a legal interest in the property, and such interest is also transferable to a third party. In many states, the investor can sell the property for a profit without actually taking title to it.

Option agreements also can be used for purchasing undeveloped real estate that is intended for development at some future time. The option locks in the purchase price for the period set forth in the agreement. In the meantime, the investor's cash can pursue more productive avenues than a property not yet ready for development—at least until the option period nears its expiration.

While options generally require a more thorough understanding of the local market in which you are working, if used correctly, they can produce a great return on the investment. The downside to options is that if you are unable to find a willing buyer within the days specified in the option, it expires and you lose the consideration fee paid to the owner. However, if you have a good understanding of the market in which you're working, you can take advantage of options with great success.

It isn't necessary to study a complex option transaction to learn the basic methodology of options. Rather, we can look at a simple option to purchase a single-family rental property at a set price with Roth IRA funds and then the subsequent exercise of the option and sale of the house for a handsome profit.

Helping Out Bob

Celia gets a call from Bob early one morning. They've had previous business dealings and spend a few minutes chatting, although Celia can't help but notice that Bob is distracted. It doesn't take long for him to come to the point. He needs $10,000 cash within two days to take care of an urgent personal matter. He explains that he hasn't been able to obtain the funds from a lender.

Celia wants to help, but she's concerned about Bob's ability to repay the money. She asks if he would be willing to put up his rental property as collateral for the loan. He agrees. The debt on the property is about $220,000.

She says she'll get back to him as soon as possible, but first she has to make a few calls. She learns from her real estate agent that, based on sales of comparable properties in the neighborhood of Bob's rental, houses are selling for $315,000 and up. Also, rental income in the area supports positive cash flow if she chooses to keep the property as a rental rather than put it up for sale.

Then Celia calls her advisor to discuss the possibility of creating an option to purchase the property using her Roth IRA. After they come up with the terms and conditions that the option agreement should contain, Celia calls Bob and presents the idea of an option investment by way of her Roth funds. He needs the money and is quick to agree.

The option agreement is drawn up for the two parties: Celia's Roth IRA at International Bank & Trust and Bob. Under its terms, Celia will have a three-month period in which to purchase the property for $220,000. She will agree to pay all expenses for the property during that period because Bob needs cash flow without expenses.

On the day following execution of the option agreement, Celia takes the agreement and her buy direction letter to International Bank & Trust, along with instructions with regard to wiring money to Bob's bank. International Bank & Trust funds the transaction that same day.

Celia has already decided to sell the property rather than keep it as a rental. If she sells the property for $300,000 or more, she can produce at least $75,000 for her Roth IRA for an investment of $10,000 plus a maximum of three months' expenses. She lists the property for $325,000.

The property sells in three weeks, not three months, and at the $325,000 selling price. Celia takes the final steps to secure her substantial profit. She exercises her option to buy Bob's outstanding mortgage. She executes a sell direction letter, sending it to International Bank & Trust, and then her Roth IRA completes the sale.

The net to Celia's Roth IRA is $302,000. The title company pays off the $220,000 loan, leaving Celia's Roth IRA $72,000 better off than it was only three weeks earlier.

Celia's Sell Direction Letter

Selling real estate that is part of your plan assets is similar to a regular real estate transaction, except that the administrator is handling it on your behalf. However, you always direct the process and approve the various transaction steps. Assets in your plan never can be sold without your permission. You can use a sell direction letter to begin the sales transaction. A typical sell direction letter includes the following information:

- The correct name and number of the account making the sale, especially if more than one account has interest in the property. You might be selling only a portion of the property and retaining proportionate interest in the other accounts.

- The property's address and location. This information is helpful in identifying the property and for documenting the sale.
- The assessor's parcel number (APN) when available. In some jurisdictions, APNs are not used, so any other assessor identification may be used instead.
- The legal description of the property to be sold, especially if there is no APN. A legal description provides the best source of identification for real property.
- The buyer's name and contact information.
- The total sales price. If at any point the sales price changes, an addendum to the letter is needed. Addenda are customary in escrow. You always should review and approve such documents.
- Information on whether the plan is financing all or part of the purchase price for the property being sold. Typically, this would be accomplished through a carry back note. Keep in mind that if the plan is financing any part of the transaction, you must complete a buy direction letter for real estate notes.
- Any escrow charges and administrative fees to be paid by the plan. Often, the allocation of escrow charges and administrative fees is negotiated between the buyer and seller and may be paid entirely by one party or shared to varying extents between buyer and seller. These costs can be important in the transaction. The instructions in the sell direction letter should be examined against the escrow instructions to ensure that your intentions are carried out properly.
- The name and contact information for the escrow agent, if any. In this way, the actual work of the closing can be completed by your designated representatives, including your administrator, escrow company, and title insurance carrier.
- Any special instructions or details regarding the transaction.

Large Return with an Option Contract

Lila has $100,000 in her Roth IRA that she rolled over from her Diamond Shamrock Pension plan to a traditional IRA and then converted to a Roth. Lila, an experienced real estate investor, is always on the lookout for appreciating properties. Her strategy is straightforward: Find a property that is undervalued, make an offer based on her knowledge of the real estate market, rehab the property, and sell it for a target profit of 25 percent, less closing costs.

Lila locates a property on which she can place a $10,000 option to purchase in consideration. The purchase price is $175,000, and it certainly qualifies as undervalued because she knows a buyer who will pay her $425,000 for it without improvements! Energized by the prospect of this once-in-a-lifetime transaction, she decides to jump-start her Roth IRA by boosting the cash from $100,000 to almost $205,750 after closing costs. This would permit her to acquire future properties or other assets in her Roth IRA without debt financing. Using her IRA funds as the consideration for the option, she is able to execute the purchase of the property and shortly thereafter sell for a profit.

Lila had her Roth IRA execute the option contract. She then had her Roth IRA enter into a sales agreement for the property with Yvonne, the buyer. Yvonne was not able to find financing for the property but had sufficient cash to pay $100,000 down. Lila, through instructions to her Roth IRA administrator, agreed to carry back a mortgage for the balance of $325,000 in Lila's Roth. Lila's Roth executed on the option contract and sold the property to Yvonne on the terms and conditions agreed to. The payments to be made to the Roth would be at 10 percent for a period of 15 years.

Lila succeeded in increasing the cash in her Roth by $100,000, also having a cash-flowing note at the same time.

Tax Lien Certificates

A tax lien certificate (TLC) documents the purchase of a tax obligation from a taxing authority. This obligation has been unpaid by the property owner of record. The taxing authority (in the following example, a county) sells the obligation to private individuals to receive immediate income. This is usually done at a public sale or auction.

By selling the certificate, the taxing authority receives the tax money it is owed, and the purchaser of the debt receives interest on the amount that is then paid. The owner of record may redeem the TLC at any time, but then also must pay interest on the obligation. The obligation may bear interest at relatively high rates, often 18 percent or more.

You can purchase obligations from a taxing authority that offers TLCs directly or by mail. This labor-intensive asset requires careful attention. The purchase amounts can be small, so many investors purchase a large number of certificates, requiring more administration needs and more cost.

In the case of auctions, the administrator can accommodate a purchase up to the amount of available cash in the account through special drafts available specifically for that purpose.

When your IRA purchases a TLC, the administrator receives the actual certificate for your benefit. This is often known as a *certificate of purchase at tax sale*. The certificate includes the purchase amount, which is remitted on your behalf to the county. The terms of the sale are also included in the certificate.

Eve Delves into Tax Lien Certificates

Eve purchases TLCs regularly at auction. She has an arrangement with her IRA administrator to get a number of cashiers' checks that she can take to an auction to purchase the TLCs for the benefit of her IRA. A purchase direction letter is used to obtain the cashiers' checks. The title is vested in the name of the IRA.

Certificates often include a sale book number. Eve always checks to make sure that the certificate number conforms to what was purchased. At a recent auction, she purchased a certificate from Polk County, Iowa. The original asset was purchased for $181, with an annual interest rate of 8 percent for four months (or 24 percent in a year).

Eve sent a buy direction letter to her administrator that provided the information needed for the administrator to send certificates for redemption. She followed up on each TLC bought and redeemed. Working together in this way lessens her administrative costs, resulting in a higher return for her plan.

AVCO Financial Services redeemed the certificate for $205. AVCO Financial Services was the beneficial owner on title for the asset. The total amount of redemption usually is included in a letter sent regarding surrendering any certificates. When a TLC is redeemed, the county sends the plan a check for the amount due. The receipt of the funds is subject to surrendering the certificate to the county treasurer.

Using Limited-Liability Corporations

A *limited-liability corporation* (LLC) is a legal form of a company offering limited liability to its owners. It is similar to a corporation but may be suitable for smaller companies with restricted numbers of owners. Its owners may be shielded from personal liability.

IRAs have invested in publicly traded stock as well as private, or closely held, stock since retirement plans and accounts began. Most of the issues regarding such ownership by IRAs center on percentages of ownership. It is necessary to ensure that these percentages comply with tax provisions. In many cases, ownership means disqualification of an individual relative to an IRA. However, disqualification in and of itself does not mean that a taxable event has occurred. If the beneficial interest owner of an LLC owned by an IRA, for example, is disqualified, it means that the entire benefit of the LLC must inure to the IRA. Once the disqualified person (the beneficial interest owner of the IRA) receives any personal benefit, the IRA ceases to be an IRA. This would be effective as of the end of the previous year in which the violation occurred. You should seek proper legal counsel and have an understanding of all requirements and potential problems involved in LLC ownership. Many individuals who follow this advice do not run into any problems. The most necessary part of any LLC is a carefully crafted document.

Most people who purchase closely held stock have no issues regarding ownership among themselves and disqualified persons. Generally, these purchases have a broad enough ownership base to ensure that a violation of percentage of ownership does not occur.

Checkbook control is often employed by people doing transactions using an LLC. A good example of this is for purchases of real estate and notes. The beneficial owner who self-directs his or her plan or IRA to purchase a controlling interest in a new LLC (not previously owned by a disqualified person) can assume an official position such as managing member or president. By doing so, the IRA is directed to have the beneficial owner be responsible for the purchases and sales within the LLC. The custodial function of the IRA is only that of the LLC. The LLC must adhere to all rules and regulations promulgated by the regulatory authorities. The IRA custodian or trustee should have no part in the formation or operation of the LLC unless the custodian wishes to be potentially considered a fiduciary or active trustee/custodian. In addition, you need to ensure that no violation of the indirect rule occurs and that unrelated business issues are dealt with.

To buy an investment property within an entity such as an LLC that is owned by an IRA or qualified plan, keep the following in mind:

- The plan or IRA can own 50 percent or more of the investment but is considered a disqualified person.
- The disqualified person cannot receive any current benefit from the investment.
- The investment must meet all IRS and Department of Labor requirements, such as prohibited transactions and tax rules.
- The investment can be debt-financed property.
- Dividends are prorated to owners based on the percentage owned.
- The investment must be constructed by competent legal counsel.

When used properly, this form of ownership can facilitate transactions effectively and easily. For an example of case law involving such transactions, refer to the landmark decision, *Swanson v. Commissioner*.

Borrowing Money

Individual retirement accounts (IRAs) and qualified plans can borrow funds, but the accounts themselves cannot be used as collateral for loans for personal use. The most difficult issue is finding a lender because the loans to purchase property must be nonrecoursive—financing where the property is the only collateral because you personally cannot be obligated to pay the note, according to the Internal Revenue Service (IRS) Code regarding trusts. A traditional loan provides for "recourse" to the borrower. In other words, if, for whatever reason, you can't make the mortgage payment, the lender reserves the right to come after you personally for the balance of the loan. In a nonrecourse loan, the cash flow from the property must be sufficient to cover the mortgage payment and all expenses because the lender cannot come back to you for any shortfalls.

Most institutional lenders won't lend to retirement plans because such loans cannot be resold in the secondary market through the usual network of mortgage bankers, brokers, and banks. Community banks and other portfolio lenders, such as hard-money or private lenders, are much more likely to make loans. Although you cannot guarantee the loan, a third party who is not related to you can. You can use other or additional collateral for the loan.

The loan-to-value (LTV) ratio is important for any lender. Banks generally lend 80 percent of the appraised property value or less on single-family dwellings. The lower the LTV ratio, the more appealing the transaction is to a lender. Private lenders or motivated sellers may lend more to your plan than banks. Also, your IRA may purchase a property subject to an existing debt.

Nonrecourse Loans

Nonrecourse loans are much like commercial loans. With commercial loans you, your credit, and your income take the back seat. The property's cash flow is the major consideration. To underwrite such a loan, the lender will request certified copies of the leases and operating expenses obtained from the seller to verify that the property can generate sufficient cash to pay the mortgage, taxes, and operating expenses. The lender also might ask for certified copies of the seller's tax returns. Rents even may be verified directly with the tenants. Once the income and expenses are determined, credits and debits are applied to come up with a net operating income (NOI) figure. The banker then will order an appraisal of the property. The appraiser determines the value of the property based on two approaches. First is the *usual-market approach*, which looks at recent resale of comparable properties. Most investors are familiar with this appraisal method. The second approach is called the *income approach*, in which the appraiser lets the lender know what the income and expenses are in the market for similar properties. IRA mortgages often have higher appraisal fees because substantially more work is being asked of the appraiser. The lender then analyzes both sets of figures—from the seller and from the appraiser—and calculates its own NOI.

Lenders often want a cushion in the expenses to cover the "extraordinary" expenses, called a *debt-service coverage ratio* (DSCR). Depending on how quickly a property could be sold in the event of default or foreclosure, the lender makes sure that the cushion is larger rather than smaller. A property such as a strip mall, which could take months to sell, typically would have a 25 percent cushion. In other words, a 10 to 25 percent cushion is left in available cash after expenses and before the lender calculates the maximum mortgage for the property.

For instance, a six-unit apartment building is being sold for $300,000. It has an NOI of $1,908 per month. The lender uses a DSCR of 1.20 for a multifamily building. The NOI of $1,908 per month is divided by 1.20, which leaves you with a figure of $1,590. This is the maximum principal and interest (P&I) that can be applied and still meet expenses and the "cushion." Using a 25-year amortization, with an interest rate of 7 percent, the maximum mortgage is $224,950. Thus, this property would require the IRA to put $75,050 (25 percent) as a down payment.

Commercial loans are also structured differently from residential loans. The most common term for a residential loan is 30 years. In commercial lending, the loan repayment schedule, or term, is 20 to 25 years. The shorter the term, the higher your monthly payment will be. Commercial loans are also commonly written as two- to five-year balloons or as adjustable-rate mortgages (ARMs). In theory, commercial loans are based on a 2.5 to 3 percent profit to the lender.

Therefore, does it make sense for your IRA to take out a loan? The answer is yes and no. The answer is yes if that is the only way the IRA can buy the property. But it might be no if the numbers don't add up. Using the example of the six-unit building, the NOI is $1,908, and the monthly P&I is $1,590. This leaves you with a positive monthly cash flow of $318 per month, or $3,816 per year. The IRA puts $75,050 into the property as a down payment. When you divide the yearly cash flow ($3,816) by the down payment, the return on investment (ROI) is 5.08 percent. The interest rate on the borrowed funds is 7 percent. Paying more for money than the rate of return is rarely prudent investing. However, you then need to consider the long term, and your answer might change to yes. Is the investment for cash flow only, or are you speculating on appreciation? If the apartment building appreciates 6 percent a year and you sell in five years, the yield and return on the IRA investment jump to almost 10.76 percent.

Finally, always make sure that you check for temporary prepayment penalties on any commercial loan. Lenders use prepayment penalties as a protection against early loan payoff, and such penalties are meant to discourage "flippers," who should be using other outlets for borrowing.

Covering a Shortage of Funds

Loan payments must be made by the retirement fund, either from the cash flow generated by the rental income or from existing funds in the account. If rental or other cash is not available, and the loan payment cannot be made, any payment made by a third party or by the IRA owner is automatically considered an excess contribution. Potentially, this may be considered a prohibited transaction. So what do you do if you need to make a loan payment or pay unexpected expenses and there's not enough money in your IRA?

- *Make a contribution to your IRA.* This is the easiest option; however, it may be used only if you haven't made a contribution at all that year or you can contribute enough funds to cover expenses without exceeding your annual contribution limit. Otherwise, it would be considered an excess contribution, with a possible penalty of 6 percent of the amount overcontributed (10 percent in the case of a SEP IRA) assessed for each year the excess contribution remains in you IRA.
- *Transfer or roll over funds from another IRA or qualified plan.* If funds are available in another plan, this is a relatively easy solution. Note that the expenses must be paid by the IRA that owns the asset, so you cannot just pay the debt from another retirement account.
- *Increase debt financing.* You may want to increase the amount of an existing loan or take out an additional one if there are more expenses than anticipated, such as for a rehab that you are planning to sell on completion. This option usually means that more points, interest, and fees have to be paid.

- *Sell another asset in your plan.* If you have another property or asset, this is an easy way to raise funds.
- *Bring in partners.* This is more complicated because it involves going through a sale process. However, after the original purchase, you cannot partner with yourself or any other disqualified persons.
- *Sell the property as is.* This option is usually the least preferable because the IRA likely would suffer a loss of the profit interest.

Unrelated Debt-Financed Income

If you borrow money to purchase an asset, the debt financing is subject to *unrelated business income tax* (UBIT). *Debt-financed property* is an IRS term for a mortgage or loan against an asset, such as real estate. You also should be aware that the account might be taxed again when you begin taking distributions, unless you're using a Roth IRA, where all withdrawals are tax-free.

Unrelated debt-financed income (UDFI) is profit made from borrowed funds. If your net income on all you debt-financed property exceeds $1,000 in a 12-month period, the portion of the debt-financed property is subject to UBIT. However, if you no longer have a debt for the property in the year prior to a sale, your plan is not subject the UBIT, regardless of the amount of profit.

UBIT must be paid by the retirement plan. You can use funds from other IRAs or plans, but first you must transfer or roll over the funds to the IRA or plan with the debt. If you pay the debt with funds not in the retirement plan, it is considered an excess contribution and may be subject to penalty.

Note that 401(k) plan acquisition debt is not subject to any other tax except when you receive funds or assets from your plan as distributions to you after age 59½ and mandatorily after age 70½. Distributions (other than substantially equal periodic withdrawals, also known as *72t distributions* permitted for IRAs only) may be subject to penalties and taxes.

Selling Debt-Financed Property

If you sell debt-financed property, you must include a percentage of any gain or loss when computing the UBIT. The percentage is that of the highest acquisition indebtedness of the property during the 12-month period preceding the date of sale in relation to the property's average adjusted basis.

The tax on this percentage of gain or loss is determined according to the usual rules for capital gains and losses. These amounts may be subject to the alternative minimum tax. If any part of the allowable capital loss is not taken into account in the current tax year, it may be carried back or carried over to another tax year without application of the debt/basis percentage for that year.

Average acquisition indebtedness is the average amount of outstanding principal debt during the part of the tax year that you hold the property. It is computed by determining how much principal debt is outstanding on the first day in each calendar month during the tax year that you hold the property, adding these amounts, and dividing the sum by the number of months during the year that you held the property. Part of a month is treated as a full month.

The *average adjusted basis* of debt-financed property is the average of the adjusted basis of the property as of the first day and as of the last day that the organization holds the property during the tax year. For example, on July 7, you buy an office building for $510,000 using $300,000 of borrowed funds, and you file your tax return on a calendar-year basis. During the year, the only adjustment to basis is $20,000 for depreciation. Starting July 28, you pay $20,000 each month on the mortgage principal plus interest. The debt/basis percentage for the year is calculated as shown in Table 6-1.

To Pay or Not to Pay: UBIT

Many people avoid investments that may incur UBIT. Or worse, they ignore the issue and hope that they won't get caught. However, being afraid of UBIT is

TABLE 6-1   Debt/Basis Percentage for the Year

July	$300,000
August	$280,000
September	$260,000
October	$240,000
November	$220,000
December	$200,000
Total for each month	$1,500,000
Average acquisition indebtedness	$1,500,000/6 months = $250,000
Basis as of July 7	$510,000
Basis as of December 31	$490,000 (due to $20,000 depreciation)
Total basis	$1,000,000
Average adjusted basis	$1,000,000/2 = $500,000

shortsighted and ignores the opportunity for building massive wealth in your retirement plan. Making an investment that may subject the IRA to UBIT is not a prohibited transaction; it just means that the IRA has to pay a tax. "But," you object, "doesn't this mean that I'm paying taxes twice?" Unless your IRA is a Roth IRA, it is true that in these two circumstances, the tax is paid by the IRA and again by the IRA holder when the income is distributed. However, the issue of double taxation is no different from investing in stocks traded on the stock exchange because corporations pay tax on income before issuing dividends to shareholders, and the value of the stock takes into account that the company must pay income taxes.

When analyzing an investment subject to UBIT, consider these two questions: "What would be the tax if I made the same transaction outside of my IRA?" The only "penalty" is the amount of tax the IRA would pay above the amount that you would pay if you had used nonretirement funds. If you make the investment personally, you would pay tax not only on the income from the investment but also on income from the next investment and the next one after that. At least within an IRA you have the choice of making investments with your proceeds that do not incur UBIT. The second question to ask is: "Will my after-UBIT return exceed what I could make on other IRA investments?" Why should you turn away from an investment in your IRA that will give you an incredible return even after paying the tax?

Here's an example of how paying UBIT might make a lot of sense. Audrey purchased a property with her Roth IRA for only $75 but subject to approximately $97,000 in delinquent taxes (for UBIT purposes, this is the same as a mortgage). The owner was willing to "give away" the property just to get rid of the headache and the lawsuit pending against him by the taxing authorities. With closing costs, the IRA spent around $3,000 to acquire the property. Only four months later, the property was sold to another investor, and the Roth IRA netted around $46,500 from the sale after paying delinquent taxes and sales expenses. Because the IRA purchased the property subject to debt (the delinquent taxes), it owed about $13,500 in UBIT on its short-term capital gain. Thus, even after paying UBIT, Audrey's IRA earned $33,000 on its $3,000 investment. This is a return of over 1,000 percent in less than four months, or an annualized return of over 4,000 percent! And since this was a Roth IRA, no more tax is owed on this income if it is distributed as a qualified distribution after age 59½ or from any other income generated in this IRA from investments that are not subject to UBIT.

Understanding and being aware of the implications of UBIT is extremely important. Review IRS Publication 598 or visit your tax advisor to get more information.

Who Pays the UBIT?

The IRA custodian is responsible for filing Form 900-T and paying the UBIT, not the owner of the IRA. The tax is paid from your IRA funds. However, the instructions for Form 990-T are not very clear. They state that the fiduciary of the IRA must file the form. The Department of Labor and the IRS have stated that the IRA owner is a fiduciary under IRS Code 4975(e)(2) because IRA owners have the right to self-direct their investments. However, the IRS has stated that IRA trustees are also fiduciaries that must demonstrate fiduciary conduct. Yet the 990-T instructions also state that the trustee of more than one IRA can file a composite Form 990-T, but the law states that an individual (e.g., an IRA owner) cannot act as trustee of an IRA. In fact, the IRS has ruled that if the IRA owner pays the UBIT, it is considered an IRA contribution. Form 990-T is not filed with your personal taxes. Instead, it is sent to the IRS in Ogden, Utah.

Avoiding UBIT

If you partner with your IRA (or qualified plan) by using IRA funds for the down payment and your personal funds for the mortgage, capital gains from a sale would be proportionately divided between you and the IRA. In this way, your IRA is not subject to UBIT because the debt financing was not incurred by the IRA. Using this approach is also a good way to get around the problem of lenders not wanting to lend to a retirement fund. Because you are partnering with yourself on an undivided interest basis, you would not be lending money to yourself. Instead, you would be an investor along with your IRA.

For example, let's say that you have a $100,000 property with a $20,000 interest vested to your IRA and $80,000 vested to you. The bank loans you the $80,000, and you personally make the payments. Any benefit from the purchase, such as rental income or income from a sale, is shared pro rata between you and the IRA. Expenses would be shared in the same way.

Bill Sidesteps UBIT

Bill Heller is a broker and is interested in purchasing additional real property for investment purposes, as well as growing his IRA. He not only wants to avoid paying UBIT, but he also would like to have an income stream that he can use now, so he decides to partner with his IRA. He currently has $400,000 in his IRA, but he knows that he shouldn't invest it all in the property because he may need funds to pay half the expenses that might arise. He finds the ideal property—a 10-unit apartment building for $750,000. Based on the net operating income of the property and cash-on-cash return, he decides that this would be a great investment for him and his IRA. He offers $720,000, which is accepted.

He splits the funding equally so that he and his IRA each own 50 percent of the investment. Rather than pay his share personally, Bill decides to take out a loan for part of the $360,000 that he owes. Because his IRA is essentially making a down payment of $360,000, it is easy for him to find a lender with a good interest rate.

Bill completes the purchase agreement in his name and his IRA. He sends his third-party administrator, IB&T, a buy direction letter with the details of the transaction. He also notifies his third-party administrator (TPA) that the title company and escrow agent will contact him to complete the transaction.

Brentwood Escrow opens the escrow account for the property and accepts an initial deposit of $72,000. The check is deposited immediately into the escrow account, and the closing is scheduled for 60 days from that point.

Bill engages American Title for this transaction and requests a preliminary title report. The TPA requests a copy of the deed from the title company and instructs the company to record it in the purchasers' names. The vesting shows a 50 percent undivided interest in the name of Bill Heller and a 50 percent undivided interest in the name of The IB&T Group, Inc., FBO Bill Heller IRA.

Prior to closing, the settlement statement provides a breakdown of the costs and charges allocated among the buyers and sellers. The earnest-money deposit is split: $36,000 remains in escrow and $36,000 is refunded to Bill Heller. The refund to Bill Heller is for the portion that his IRA has an interest in. If that portion had not been refunded to Bill, it would have been considered an excess contribution. Bill arranges for the lender to pay for the remainder of his share, totaling $324,000, and he personally pays for his share of the closing costs.

The rental agreements for the apartments are assigned to Bill and his plan equally. At closing, Bill requests the renters to make all checks out to his IRA and mail them to IB&T. IB&T deposits half the amount in Bill's plan and writes Bill a check for the other half. That check is not written from his IRA but from a separate account maintained for this purpose. Because Bill owns the apartment building with his IRA, he does not do any of the maintenance or property management himself to avoid prohibited transactions. Any bills for services are sent to IB&T, which then divides the payments proportionately between Bill and the IRA. However, all mortgage payments are paid exclusively by Bill.

If Bill decides to sell the property in a few years, half the proceeds would belong to his IRA and would not be subject to any UBIT because that portion had not been debt financed. Bill's half of the profits would be subject to any tax that would be applicable if he were to sell any property that he personally owned.

"Subject to" Purchases

You can debt finance a "subject to" purchase, which refers to buying a property that is subject to an existing debt. In some cases, the loan on the property may be assumed by the buyer. In other cases, the lender accelerates the loan so that it can be paid off when the property is sold.

Some states have laws governing "subject to" loans and assumptions by buyers. The IRS Code specifies that "subject to" loans are also subject to the tax on unrelated debt-financed income and are therefore taxable on a prorated basis in IRAs, 401(k)s, and qualified plans in general.

Darren Buys Out Ken

Darren is experienced in purchasing "subject to" properties. He hears that Ken, who owns a desirable property, needs to move out of state for personal reasons and doesn't want to continue making the monthly mortgage payment.

The amount owed on the property is $167,000, with a monthly expense of $1,083, which includes mortgage, taxes, insurance, and homeowner's association dues. Comparable properties in the area are selling at $285,000. Darren figures that he can make about $100,000 after expenses if he sells the property right away.

If Darren decides to hold onto the property, other important considerations are also on the positive side of his ledger. He estimates that he can rent out the property for $1,200 to $1,300 a month. Furthermore, the homeowner's association has been discussing transforming the area into a gated community, which would increase the value of the property. If he holds the property, Darren's income after debt carry (loan interest and principal payments) would be about $2,000 annually, with the property continuing to appreciate.

Ken wants to do the deal quickly because he needs money soon to establish himself in another state and to pay off some lingering credit-card debt. Ken is happy to walk away with $20,000 in cash. Darren realizes that the existing 6 percent fixed-rate loan for 15 years is a great deal for him. Thus Darren tells Ken that he will cash him out and take over the payments by paying the lender directly. Darren informs the lender that he will be making the payments. Darren's Roth IRA also could have leased the property from Ken and could have executed an option agreement to purchase the property.

Darren now has to decide how to fund it. His traditional IRA contains more than enough cash to buy the property outright from Ken, with Ken remaining on the title but grant-deeding the property to Darren. But Darren, who is self-employed, knows that his modified adjusted gross income (AGI) will not exceed the allowable amount for that year, so he realizes that it's a good time to convert at least some of his traditional IRA funds to Roth IRA funds. He has had a self-directed IRA for many years, and using his Roth IRA for the transaction with Ken fits nicely into Darren's long-term financial goal—to make a lot of money tax-free!

Darren decides to move $40,000 of his traditional IRA cash into a Roth IRA. To preserve the entire amount, he uses his personal funds to pay the tax on the conversion rather than his IRA funds. Even if the house remains vacant, the $40,000 will cover the cost of acquisition from Ken, plus one year of mortgage, tax, insurance payments, and potential repair costs. Darren has many other rentals in his IRA and knows that all expenses associated with IRA-owned property are borne by the IRA.

Here is Darren's transaction a step at a time:

Step 1: Darren withdraws $40,000 from his traditional self-directed IRA and makes a "conversion contribution" to a self-directed Roth IRA at EntrustUSA. Although Darren has 60 days to make the conversion without penalty, he is able to do it within a day because his traditional IRA is also with EntrustUSA. This conversion amount will be included as income on his tax return for the year, but thanks to excellent tax planning by Darren and his tax accountant, the tax will not exceed the estimated tax he has already paid.

Step 2: Darren prepares a purchase agreement for Ken's property, which shows the buyer as Darren's Roth IRA. Ken will remain on the loan for the property, and Darren's Roth IRA will make the payments to the lender. The Roth IRA pays Ken $20,000, and Ken grant-deeds the property to Darren's Roth IRA. Ken agrees to pay a monthly rent of $1,083 for as long as he occupies the property because he knows a big cash payment is heading his way, and he plans to leave the state soon.

Step 3: Darren prepares a buy direction letter and sends it along with the contract to EntrustUSA. Escrow is opened at Darren's attorney's office, as agreed to by Ken. The attorney writes up the grant deed. A settlement document is sent to EntrustUSA. The funding amount, plus fees, totals $22,000— $20,000 to Ken plus $2,000 in closing fees. Ken agrees to pay half the $2,000 closing fees.

Because the lender knows both Darren and Ken, the lender is happy to retain Ken as the borrower and to permit Darren's Roth IRA to pay the loan. The grant deed is recorded, and the Roth IRA now owns the property "subject to" the loan being paid by Ken. Should Darren's IRA fail to make the payments, Ken will be responsible for the payments on the loan, but he also will then own the property.

Step 4: Darren had been advised years ago that debt-financed property is subject to UBIT tax. His tax accountant, who is an expert in UBIT, has filed Form 990-T, Exempt Organization Business Income Tax Return (Schedule E of the form deals with UBIT), for some of Darren's other properties. Bill prepares Form 990-T, which, in turn, is signed by an authorized representative of EntrustUSA and sent to the IRS.

Step 5: Darren decides that rather than sell the property, he will keep it and rent it out. While Ken prepares to move out of the state, he gives Darren the go-ahead to look for a new tenant. Although there are many interested parties, Darren's standards for renters are not met by the time the transaction closes. A month later, Ken takes his $19,000 ($1,000 covering his share of the closing fees) and leaves for his new home after paying Darren's Roth IRA $1,083 for a month's rent.

Darren's Roth IRA now has a property to rent and mortgage and property expenses to pay. Because he has had vacancies on properties before, Darren makes sure that the Roth can handle the mortgage for an extended period of time, if necessary. Since he is still within the year when his modified AGI is less than the allowable amount, he can convert additional funds if he needs to.

Step 6: After three months, Darren locates a suitable renter, Greg, through ads placed in the local paper. The ads are paid for by his Roth IRA. Greg likes the property and is happy to enter into a rental agreement at $1,200 per month for one year with the Roth IRA. The contract calls for a security deposit of $2,400 to cover first and last month rents. It also requires an additional deposit of $1,200 to cover Greg's dogs, Dusty and Abe. The total deposit of $3,600 is placed into Darren's Roth IRA in an FDIC-insured account. The rental contract is read and approved by Darren and executed by EntrustUSA.

To summarize, Darren's Roth IRA now owns a $285,000 property, which he purchased for $21,000 and for which property cash flowed after three months. If he wishes, Darren can sell the property and make almost $100,000 in immediate profit for his Roth. Because the market is still expanding, he decides to have the Roth rent it out for a year. Then he'll check back in on his investment and determine its future course.

A word of caution: Keep in mind that insurance on vacant property is usually expensive partly because of the risks involved to the insurer.

Getting into the Lending Business

If you are not interested in managing property or personally buying and selling real estate, loaning your funds to others is a good way to go because the property can serve as collateral. You can loan your retirement funds to individuals and businesses as long as you do not violate the rules on prohibited transactions (see Chapter 9). You cannot make loans to yourself or to family members who are ascendants or descendants. However, you can make loans to your siblings under certain circumstances. There are no guidelines regarding the interest rates you can charge (or not charge).

The loans can be secured or unsecured as long as you are not the one personally securing the loan. And don't even think about loaning the funds to a third party who then loans the funds to you—this is considered self-dealing and is a violation.

Irene's IRA Goes into the Lending Business

At age 35, Irene decides to go out on her own and start up a financial consulting business. She takes the $300,000 from the 401(k) she had with her former employer and rolls it into a traditional IRA. Regarding future annual contributions to her retirement, she plans a three-pronged approach: $15,000 for her Roth 401(k) deferral, $15,000 into her tax-deferred simplified employee pension (SEP) IRA from her consulting practice (where she is both employer and an employee), and $4,000 for her Roth IRA. In other words, she intends to add to her retirement by $34,000 in that first year of self-employment.

Irene doesn't want to stop there. She has a growing interest in real estate but little interest in the day-to-day operational stresses of being a landlord. Turning her IRA into a lender, on the other hand, is right up her alley, considering her financial knowledge and experience. Through her connections with real estate brokers and sales associates, she knows that there are a lot of people who want to borrow money for a home purchase but who lack the credit scores to qualify for loans through institutional lenders. Most of them fall into at least one of three categories: young, no borrowing history, and previous credit problems.

Before Irene's IRA makes a single real estate loan, she realizes that she must come up with a set of standards around the following issues: Who will she lend to? For what purpose? How much will she lend? For how long and at what rate? What kind of collateral will she demand?

Who will she lend to? Her first priority is to investigate the potential borrower's credit history so that she can get an idea of the credit risk involved. A credit history provides details about a person's current income sources and current monthly payments. Just as important, it shines a light on past financial responsibility, such as the level of debt carried, whether there has been a recent bankruptcy or family crisis that caused problems with traditional lenders, and whether there has been a history of getting overextended.

For what purpose? Irene decides that she is most interested in borrowers who have something to lose if they fail to make loan payments to her IRA. She particularly likes prospective first-time homebuyers who have been saving for a down payment and presumably taking pains to build a good credit history and who have a great deal to lose—namely, their home.

How much will she lend? In Irene's middle-class community, a two-bedroom, two-bath starter home customarily sells for around $125,000. Therefore, her IRA could make two loans based on that price point. She decides that she will make loans on properties that have a maximum loan-to-value (LTV) ratio of 80 percent, which means that the borrowers will have to come up with 20 percent down payment and closing costs, or about $30,000. Borrowers who put this amount of money into their home purchase likely will be serious about keeping up with loan payments.

For how long and at what rate? Irene considers a 30-year fixed-rate loan at 10 percent. For a $100,000 loan, in addition to the principal balance, the return to Irene's IRA would be $215,926 after 30 years; on adjusting for 2 percent inflation, the return would be $164,155. In other words, if her IRA made two such $100,000 loans in the first year, after 30 years it would be sitting pretty with $630,000, or $528,000 when adjusted for 2 percent inflation.

What kind of collateral will she demand? Irene decides that she is willing to go through the process of foreclosure and sell the property to recapture her investment.

Now that she has come up with a solid set of standards to govern her lending transactions, Irene is definitely excited about the potential of her venture. Thanks to the power of compounding, and because she plans to reinvest the principal and interest income in future loans, she believes that in 30 years her original IRA investment of $200,000 can grow to $3.4 million (or over $2 million when adjusted for inflation). And after factoring in her annual contributions (beginning with the $34,000 she contributed this year), by age 65, she will have a retirement portfolio in the several millions.

This is pretty heady stuff, but Irene knows the reality lurking in real estate loans—the risk of default. To mitigate that risk, she decides that borrowers must be employed. If the borrowers are a married couple and both of them work, she takes a look at what might happen if one or the other loses his or her job. She is aware that the number of bankruptcies that result after one spouse becomes unemployed is surprisingly high. Many couples with two incomes raise their lifestyle expectations without considering what might happen if one of them suddenly loses his or her job.

Irene also needs to study the real estate market. What would happen if there is a downturn in the economy? If the real estate market goes flat? If interest rates fall and borrowers can qualify for a lower loan rate?

Nonetheless, Irene is not deterred. She knows that these kinds of transactions aren't as rock steady as a Treasury bond with a 10 percent return cash on cash. But she believes that the real estate market in her area is sufficiently buoyant; at the very least, she won't lose her principal. Further, she is confident, based on her set of lending standards, that she will end up with borrowers who will be adequately equipped to handle the inevitable economic ups and downs. Lastly, as a conscientious risk mitigator, she plans to use only the funds from her original 401(k) plan that she rolled into an IRA, reserving the funds from her tax-free and tax-deferred accounts to help her ride out any temporary crises and providing liquid cash for less risky investments.

Building toward a Comfortable Retirement

Paul has discovered his mortality. He, like so many others, has not saved diligently toward retirement, and now at age 50 he finds himself with only $100,000 in a traditional IRA. What else does he have? His own small business, but he's not in a line of work that will bring in a significant amount when he sells it. He also has two rental houses free and clear, with a combined market value of $600,000; a personal residence worth $750,000, which still has a mortgage; and a desire to retire at age 60. This desire is also shared by his wife, Janet, who also is 50 but without any retirement savings.

Paul and Janet come up with a plan. They can move into one of their rental houses, which is already paid off. Then they can sell their personal residence and pay off the mortgage, anticipating a $500,000 tax-free profit from the sale by taking advantage of the home exclusion allowance. This would put them in the following pretax position:

Paul's traditional IRA: $100,000
Janet's IRA: $0
Cash for investment: $500,000
Rental property: $300,000 (the other rental becoming their primary residence)

If they invest Paul's $100,000 IRA in mutual funds, his return might be about $7,000 per year, tax deferred. Putting the $500,000 from the sale of their home in mutual funds could add about $35,000 per year—about $28,000 after tax. The rental property currently brings in about $12,000 per year after expenses. In other words, if Paul and Janet want to retire in about 10 years, and assuming that they live at least 20 years beyond that—which means they're looking at 30 years of living expenses plus inflationary pressures—they realize that they need to take action in the next decade to make their retirement hopes affordable.

Paul's first move is to establish a self-directed profit-sharing Roth 401(k) for his small business, which employs Janet, their daughter Lucille (age 25), and two others. He intends to maximize his Roth 401(k) contribution, putting in $15,000 plus the $5,000 allowable catch-up each year. Janet also will maximize her deferral at Paul's level ($15,000 plus $5,000). Paul and Janet will make employer contributions to the three employees (including Lucille), with a net of 5 percent each from modified adjusted gross income, or $8,000 for Paul and $8,000 for Janet, into their tax-deferred employer contribution account. Because Paul and Janet make more than $160,000 per year, they cannot contribute to Roth IRAs. Instead, they will contribute $4,500 each to traditional IRAs.

After carrying out their plan faithfully for a year, here is where Paul and Janet find themselves:

Paul's traditional IRA: $104,500
Janet's traditional IRA: $4,500

Paul's Roth 401(k): $20,000 ($15,000 maximum plus $5,000 catch-up)

Janet's Roth 401(k): $20,000 ($15,000 maximum plus $5,000 catch-up)

Paul's contributory (tax-deferred) profit-sharing Roth 401(k): $8,000

Janet's contributory (tax-deferred) profit-sharing Roth 401(k): $8,000

This adds up to $165,000 in tax-deferred and tax-free retirement accounts.

Paul and Janet's goal is to end up with $100,000 per year in tax-free income by the time they reach age 60. Using a conservative estimate, they will need to put away $2.5 million. But based on the current amount that they have— $500,000 from the sale of their home, rental property worth $300,000, and $165,000 in retirement funds—they will fall short by nearly a million (assuming that they don't make anything on their investments). Thus, although they will be tightening their belts, the investment in their future is now necessary.

At their age they don't want to take any huge risks; they'll leave that kind of gambling to the younger crowd. Paul has lost significant money in the stock market in the past and is not comfortable putting a big stake in that arena again. What about real estate? They both have some experience, having owned two rental homes, one of which they now live in. They have a number of friends who are in commercial real estate, developing properties such as housing tracts and strip centers. Nonetheless, they don't want to invest directly in real estate, and they're not interested in managing properties either.

They remember Bruce, a friend who has been a success in the commercial real estate construction business for many years. Only once did a project go poorly for Bruce, causing him to buy out his investors. Paul and Janet feel confident that making building loans to Bruce, who dependably pays 8 percent interest, would be a smart investment. And with $165,000 in tax-free and tax-deferred accounts available to them, as well as the $500,000 from the home sale, they have $665,000 at the ready.

Paul and Janet approach Bruce with their intentions, and he's happy to have them on board. Now committed to going ahead with their investment, they combine their IRAs and 401(k)s for the purpose of making building loans. The

Entrust Group, with more than 25 years of experience in self-directed plans, is their 401(k) sponsor and record keeper.

The neophyte building lenders approach their new responsibilities with care. Paul and Janet read and approve all necessary documents. Thanks to Bruce's good relationships with the title and escrow companies, the process is seamless. Funding via Entrust is also straightforward. For the 401(k)s, Paul and Janet are cotrustees of the plan, which simplifies matters. Some of their building investments are done jointly with their 401(k)s and IRAs, whereas other projects are done separately by the various accounts. The couple makes sure to invest tax-free account funds first, particularly on any loans that hold a promise of a return above 8 percent.

All income and expenses for the 401(k) and IRA accounts are allocated according to the percentage of participation of the respective accounts. Considering the variety of accounts—tax-deferred, tax-free, and employer contribution—every effort is made by Entrust to maintain proper record keeping. Additionally, Entrust sends the trust accounting to the 401(k) plan administrator each year to facilitate preparation of the annual 5500 tax return.

Now let's see where Paul and Janet could be at age 60. Their 401(k) and IRA portfolios would be worth $356,000 without adding another penny, but if they maximized their contributions every year at current rates, the value of those portfolios would jump to $856,000. Adding that to their investment returns from their original capital of $500,000 (from the home sale) would get them close to $2 million. If their rental home increases in value over 10 years to $500,000, their formerly distant goal of $2.5 million now looks completely within reach. And keep in mind that this is a conservative estimate, with an investment growth of only 4 percent annually.

When they do reach age 60, Paul and Janet will have met their target income of $100,000 for retirement easily. They won't have to worry about mandatory distributions from their tax-deferred accounts until they are 70½. The Roth portion of their portfolios does not have a mandatory distribution date. Just as they managed their money responsibly in their fifties to provide for a comfortable retirement, once they retire, they must obtain sound financial advice about the current tax laws to figure out which money they should withdraw and when.

Byron Helps Out

Jack, a real estate broker, has a client with a $200,000 property that's been languishing on the market for more than a year. At last, there may be good news on the horizon: a potential buyer, Emma, has placed the property under contract. But it's not clear sailing yet. Her loan is only for $160,000, which is $15,000 short. Because Emma has not worked for the past two years, the lender balks at increasing the loan amount. Now Jack is worried that the deal is going to fall through.

Fortunately, he remembers Byron, the real estate broker who works across the hall. Jack knows that Byron is always on the lookout for making loans to fellow brokers' clients. He catches up to him at the water cooler and tells him about Emma and the property. Byron likes what he hears, and introductions soon follow.

Byron has a self-directed SEP IRA with Entrust, to which he contributes each year. His current balance is around $250,000. He realizes that while he can handle negotiations related to Emma's loan situation, his IRA administrator is the only one who can sign the loan documents. He also is aware that loans have risk and that he is responsible for assessing the risk and pricing the loan; the IRA administrator doesn't provide investment advice.

After doing his research, Byron presents Emma with two options: (1) a $175,000 first mortgage on the property with a 30-year amortization at a fixed rate of 7.825 percent (slightly higher than the bank's rate) and one point or (2) a $16,000 second mortgage on the property with a rate of 8 percent, a $500 fee, and interest-only payments for three years, at which time the loan comes due.

Emma is not comfortable with the idea of a three-year balloon payment, so she chooses Byron's first option. She's worried about coming up with the cash to pay the point though, so she asks him to increase the loan to $178,000 and pay the point out of the proceeds. Byron offers to make it easier for her: He decreases the point from 1 to ¾ and keeps the balance at $178,000. Emma agrees.

Byron proceeds to do what a lender usually does. He directs his title company to prepare the loan documents, listing the lender as his SEP IRA, Entrust, FBO Byron IRA. He then contacts ABC Administration with instructions for funding the closing. He makes sure that the loan is recorded properly. The trust deed secures the note with the property. The insurance for the property is in place. Entrust, FBO Byron IRA is listed as loss payee for up to the amount of the loan. ABC Administration sends $176,665 to the closing ($178,000 less its fee of $1,335).

During the ensuing months, Emma mails her payments to Byron in a timely manner, payable to Entrust, FBO Byron IRA. Byron tracks the interest and principal before sending the check on to Entrust. He has chosen to do the tracking himself instead of hiring a loan-servicing company. Such a company typically would have recorded payments and sent them on to the IRA administrator, as well as handled notices and other reporting to the borrower.

Six months after the initial transaction, Emma has found a job, and her credit rating is improving. Byron decides to sell the note to another lender, Note Servicing, Inc. Note Servicing evaluates the loan, which now has a balance of $177,245. It determines that the loan has a market value of about 6.75 percent but agrees to buy it at an interest rate of 7.125 percent. Since the note is paying interest at 7.825 percent, the value of the note, $189,722, is more than its balance. Note Servicing pays the value to Entrust, FBO Byron IRA, which at Byron's instruction promptly assigns the note to Note Servicing.

So how did all of this play out for Byron's SEP IRA? Very well indeed. His IRA invested $176,665 and received back $189,722 plus six monthly payments totaling $7,706 less expenses of $295 for the transactions paid to ABC Administration. In other words, his IRA grew $20,468 richer in only six months, a net gain of 11 percent.

Byron, now with $270,000 in his SEP IRA, again is making the rounds to his fellow brokers, reminding them that he's the man to approach when there's a client having trouble getting a loan.

Sam Seeks a Quick Profit: Investing in a Preconstruction Project

Sam is scouting around for a good short-term investment return for cash in his traditional IRA. He doesn't have a lot to invest, and he's not impressed with the returns in the equity and bond markets. Sam, who is 50 years old, is comfortable with taking some risk, so when Harold, a builder he knows, approaches him with an intriguing preconstruction opportunity, he goes for it. Harold needs $23,500 in cash, with the balance of the project (about $185,000) to be covered by a loan from a hard-money lender. Once the property is built, Sam will have two options: He can buy it and use it as a long-term income property or have Harold sell it and be repaid from the net profit.

Sam negotiates for the take-out option with his mortgage broker, Renee, keeping his options open to perhaps own the property and rent it out for long-term cash flow. He directs his IRA administrator to put additional cash into the transaction when it comes time to have the IRA borrow the money. The amount of cash required is $150,000, which is the amount of the loan Sam's IRA will need. Because Sam is using his IRA, he needs to obtain nonrecourse financing (financing where the property is the only collateral, and Sam will not be obligated on the note) for the take-out portion. Renee is not able to find a portfolio lender to finance the final acquisition or take-out of the home on completion for the IRA. Sam decides to go ahead anyway. He structures the transaction for his IRA to lend Harold $23,500 on an unsecured basis. The loan is to be repaid from the net proceeds of the sale of the completed building. The division of the profits will be 25 percent to Sam and the rest to Harold. The home sold for $285,000. After the loan expense of $14,535, construction and closing costs, the profit was

$68,815. Sam received 25 percent of that—$17,204—on $23,500 invested for a nine-month period.

Sam Needs to Decide: Traditional or Roth IRA

When Sam loaned Harold money for the construction project, he used funds from his traditional IRA. What if Sam had tapped a Roth IRA rather than a traditional IRA for his preconstruction investment? To keep the comparison straightforward, let's assume that the amount invested is the same ($23,500), the rate of return from the construction loan is 6 percent over the next 20 years, and Sam doesn't make additional contributions to his Roth IRA.

First, let's look at the up-front tax consequences. In contrast to traditional IRA contributions, which are tax deductible in the year that they are made, Roth IRA contributions are not tax deductible, but the distributions are tax-free. Assuming that Sam's tax rate is 35 percent, he has paid $8,225 in tax on $23,500 in Roth contributions; in other words, he has $8,225 less to invest. In contrast, Sam didn't have to pay tax on his traditional IRA, and he wisely invested the $8,225 in a 7 percent certificate of deposit (CD).

Whether the funds for the loan came from a Roth or traditional IRA, Sam's preconstruction investment profit of $17,204 is the same. After adding the profit to the repaid principal of $23,500, both IRAs would have $40,704. However, in Sam's Roth IRA, that $40,704 and any additional profits from it would not be taxed on distribution at or after age 59½. In a traditional IRA, the same amount and additional profits would be taxed at the tax rate Sam would pay for distributions.

So let's see how this works. For the sake of this example, Sam invests the $40,704 in a CD earning 7 percent. After 20 years, his investment has grown to $168,537. Since Sam is now 59½ years old, he decides to take a lump-sum distribution of the full amount. From his traditional IRA, assuming a tax rate of 20 percent, Sam receives $134,830. But he also has the $8,225 he saved in taxes that he put into a 7 percent CD compounding annually. Despite annual tax payments on that investment income at Sam's tax rate of 35 percent, it has grown to $21,429. So he now has an after-tax total of $156,259. In contrast, the Roth IRA produces a tax-free distribution of $168,537—that's a $12,279 difference in Sam's favor!

If Sam doesn't choose to take a lump-sum distribution, he would be required to take a distribution from his traditional IRA at age 70½, but he's not required to take one from his Roth IRA, which is something that is very important to consider. IRS statistics show that a 70-year-old will live an additional 21 years. In addition, about 27 percent of individuals continue to work and earn income after reaching the legal retirement age, although at age 70½, a person is no longer permitted to contribute to an IRA. In this scenario, if Sam were to continue to work, his tax rate could be higher than 20 percent, thereby further reducing his earnings from his traditional IRA.

C H A P T E R

Asset Protection

The 2005 U.S. Supreme Court decision in *Rousey v. Jacoway* implies that individual retirement accounts (IRAs) now are afforded protection in bankruptcy; however, it is not exactly clear that the new ruling fully excludes IRAs from bankruptcy estates.

The debtors argued that Section 522(d)(10)(E) of the Bankruptcy Code protected their IRA assets from the claims of their creditors. That section applies to protecting "retirement assets" if three tests are met:

1. The right to receive the payment is from a "stock bonus, pension, profit sharing, annuity, or similar plan or contract."
2. The right to receive payment is "on account of illness, disability, death, age, or length of service."
3. The right to receive payment is withheld from the bankruptcy estate only to the extent that it is "reasonably necessary to support" the debtor and/or his or her dependents.

Since application of the third test was not before the Supreme Court in *Rousey*, the Court focused on whether the first two tests were met. In ruling that the first test was met, the Court found IRAs to be "similar plans or contracts within the meaning of Section 522(d)(10(e).” The Court then found that the second test was met because the 10 percent penalty imposed for distributions from an IRA prior to age 59½ is a “substantial barrier” to early withdrawal and thus provides “a right to payment on account of age.” The third test was remanded to the Court of Appeals for a determination. To fully exempt their IRA from their bankruptcy estate, the Rouseys now have to prove that their IRA funds are “reasonably necessary to support” themselves and their dependents.

Rousey does not clearly mean that IRAs are completely exempt from a debtor’s bankruptcy estate. The third item in the three-part test states that an IRA is exempt only to the extent that the funds are reasonably necessary for the support of the debtor and his or her dependents. If only two-thirds of the IRA funds are necessary for support, the remaining third is not eligible for the exemption and therefore remains subject to the claims of creditors as part of the bankruptcy estate. It’s possible that the *Rousey* decision therefore is of limited value to wealthy IRA holders.

Rousey is irrelevant to IRA holders who live in states that preclude debtors from using the Section 522(d) exemptions. The ruling is also irrelevant to IRA holders who live in states that provide debtors with the option of applying state rather than federal exemptions, and the state exemptions are broader. In addition, *Rousey* does not change existing law for states such as California, where IRAs are already exempt from the claims of creditors to the extent reasonably necessary to support the IRA holder and his or her dependents.

Keep this in mind if you are considering rolling over assets from an Employee Retirement Income Act (ERISA) plan to an IRA because neither the *Rousey* case nor any state laws provide protection from creditors equal to the absolute exclusion extended to ERISA plans under the Bankruptcy Code.

Beyond the Reach of Creditors

Ernest participated in the company profit-sharing plan and regularly made 401(k) contributions during his tenure at Galactic Enterprises, Inc. When he left the company, he had accrued over $100,000 in his retirement account. A friend told Ernest about self-directed retirement plans, which gave him the ability to freely choose his retirement account investments. So he rolled his 401(k) assets over to a self-directed IRA. This strategy expanded Ernest's investment choices to include real estate, limited-liability companies, partnerships, private placements, discounted notes, lending, and a whole host of alternative opportunities.

Unlike Ernest, his father, Darrell, had not bothered with a retirement plan, thinking that having savings was enough. He had remarried, and his new wife had over $100,000 in savings. Ernest and Darrell decided to partner on some local real estate investments. They found a duplex in town for $200,000. They each contributed $100,000—Ernest had his IRA buy it, and Darrell used his wife's personal funds. Ernest's custodian took title to an undivided 50 percent interest in the duplex for the benefit of Ernest's IRA. Darrell and his wife took title to the remaining 50 percent interest. The duplex generated a positive cash flow of $10,000 per year—$5,000 each. Ernest's IRA enjoyed tax-favored status and thus realized no current tax liability. Darrell was able to take the normal investment real estate deductions to reduce or eliminate his tax liability on the annual income.

The real estate market was heating up in their area. They anticipated doubling their money within the next three to five years. If they each realized a $100,000 profit, however, the investors would experience completely divergent outcomes. The IRA's gain would be tax-deferred until Ernest started taking distributions at retirement age. The entire equity would continue to build Ernest's future retirement reserve. Darrell, unless he initiated a 1031 exchange, would recognize the full gain in the year of the sale and lose between 15 and 25 percent to federal income taxes. (If they sold the duplex in less than one year from the date of acquisition, Darrell would be taxed at the short-term capital gain rate of up to 35 percent.)

Unfortunately, calamity struck before the proverbial ship came in. Unbeknownst to Ernest and Darrell, the electrical system in the duplex was faulty. One morning, a toaster full of Pop-Tarts blew out the electrical panel in

Unit A and caused a ferocious fire. A caustic chain reaction engulfed Unit B in flames and took the life of one of the tenants. The ensuing wrongful death lawsuit resulted in a judgment totaling almost $3 million! (Fortunately, the duplex was insured, so insurance proceeds were used to restore the duplex at replacement cost.)

Here's where Ernest's diligence really paid off. Asset protection for retirement plans is derived from a variety of sources. ERISA protects assets held in qualified plans (generally employer-sponsored plans) from legal process, provided that the plan document contains the prescribed "antialienation" provisions. In addition, the Bankruptcy Code excludes the qualified plan assets from a bankrupt's estate. ERISA does not protect assets held in IRAs from creditor claims, however. But several states have statutes that exempt retirement plan assets, including those held in IRAs, from legal process. And thanks to recent court cases and changes in the Bankruptcy Code, assets held in retirement plans, including IRAs, are effectively shielded from creditor claims. The recent decision of the U.S. Supreme Court in *Rousey v. Jacoway* ruled that the IRAs held by debtors in bankruptcy, under the facts of that case, were exempt from the reach of their creditors. This decision may have limited application, however. The better news for IRA holders is that the Bankruptcy Code itself has been amended (effective October 17, 2005) to exempt all IRAs from the reach of creditors when an IRA holder becomes a debtor in bankruptcy.

Because Ernest's 50 percent interest in the duplex was held inside the IRA, both Ernest and the duplex are insulated from the legal process initiated to collect on the judgment. By virtue of the state statute and U.S. Bankruptcy Code protections, an impenetrable barrier repels a judgment creditor trying to reach inside a plan and grab assets to satisfy the judgment. The retirement plan trust (in this instance, the IRA) owned the duplex, so Ernest was not personally implicated in the duplex-related enterprise. Both the benefits and liabilities were exclusively within the province of the IRA. In other words, the claimants had to sue the IRA custodian, as trustee, not Ernest, to obtain a judgment in the first place. Only his IRA assets, not his personal assets, were potentially exposed to the claims. However, following the entry of a judgment against the IRA, a road-block bars the creditor from executing against the duplex because it is an asset of the IRA and exempt from legal process. Ernest's retirement plan assets lay beyond the reach of creditors.

Darrell did not fare as well. His duplex investment was made with personal funds; Darrell and his wife held title personally. The judgment creditors had a field day going after Darrell's 50 percent interest in the duplex and then proceeded to execute against their remaining personal assets. Darrell filed bankruptcy but still ended up with only the 1988 Buick and the gold cufflinks Grandma had given him. The diligent retirement planner is wise to hold real estate and other assets inside his or her IRA or 401(k) plan. Not only does this strategy lead to profit, but it also serves to preserve the assets amassed over a lifetime of investing.

Prohibited Transactions

As you can see from the examples in this book, there are many kinds of opportunities that you can take advantage of to grow your retirement funds. However, there are certain transactions that you cannot do or that should be avoided. The rules for prohibited transactions are outlined in Section 4975 of the Internal Revenue Service (IRS) Code (see the Appendix). A prohibited transaction is any improper use of a retirement plan by the plan participant or any disqualified person, either directly or indirectly. The following are considered disqualified persons:

- A fiduciary of the plan (this includes yourself and any advisors, such as the custodian or third-party administrator)
- Your spouse
- Lineal ascendants and descendants and their spouses (i.e., grandparents, parents, and children)
- An employer of any of the participants in a plan
- A person providing services to the plan

- Corporations, partnerships, trusts, or estates in which you own at least 50 percent of the total voting stock, directly or indirectly

There are two separate and distinct ways in which any given transaction can violate the prohibited transaction rules. First, there is the transaction itself, such as selling a property or making a loan. Second, there is the decision by the fiduciary to have the plan enter into the transaction. The fiduciary conflict-of-interest provisions often are the ones that get many people into trouble.

Fiduciaries of retirement plans owe a duty of undivided loyalty to the plans for which they act. Thus the prohibitions are to deter them from taking advantage of the authority, control, and responsibility that they have. Any action taken where there is a conflict of interest or a direct benefit that may affect the fiduciary's best judgment is likely to be prohibited.

For example, if Mary Sloan, a fiduciary of the ABC company plan who has authority to manage the plan, retains her son, Bennett Sloan, to provide for a fee various kinds of administrative services necessary for operation of the plan, Mary is engaged in a prohibitive action because Bennett has an interest that may affect Mary's best judgment as a fiduciary.

In the same way, since you are considered the fiduciary of your retirement account, you may receive reasonable fees for managing the assets, much like a portfolio manager, but you cannot be reimbursed for actual property management or repairs, and even "sweat" equity and donating materials could be considered an excess contribution as well as a prohibited transaction.

If you engage in a prohibited transaction with your retirement plan, you risk losing the tax exemption, and you must include the value of your account in your gross income for that taxable year. If you pledge any portion of your funds as collateral for a loan, the amount pledged is treated as a distribution and must be included in your gross income for that year.

Because it is simply not worth engaging in prohibited actions, let's look at some examples.

Prohibited Transactions between Disqualified Persons

Transferring a retirement plan's income or assets to a disqualified person, or allowing them to be used by a disqualified person, is a prohibited transaction. Your plan cannot sell, exchange, or lease property to a disqualified person. Nor can it lend money or furnish goods or services.

Although the IRS Code states that disqualified persons include ascendants, descendants, and their spouses, it's better not to push the envelope. Because the IRS also has issues with people who may influence the decisions of the owner of an individual retirement account (IRA) or qualified plan, it's best to avoid dealing with siblings or other relatives who might be viewed as having direct influence for their benefit. Think twice, therefore, before having your IRA make a loan to a relative who wants to purchase a home.

There Is No Free Rent

Joe and Kate, a married couple, each has an IRA. They decide that a single-family rental property would fit nicely into their retirement portfolios. Although each IRA has sufficient funds to cover the purchase individually, Joe and Kate want income for both IRAs. They complete the necessary documentation to direct International Bank and Trust, as custodian, to purchase the rental property for an undivided 50 percent interest for each IRA.

During the first year, everything goes fine. They find a renter who is willing to sign a year-to-year rental agreement (with a 5 percent annual increase). The monthly rent of $1,500 is divided 50/50, or $750 to each of Joe and Kate's IRAs. With an annual real estate tax payment of $3,020 and maintenance of $1,000 a year, each IRA pays out $2,010. Joe and Kate's cash return of 8 percent is in line with their income projections, and meanwhile, they are aware that properties in the area of their rental are appreciating.

After another solid year of income and continuing appreciation, their tenant decides to take a job in another state. They instruct their IRAs to advertise for renters, but three months go by without a taker. Just as they begin to get uncomfortable with the cash drain on their IRAs, their daughter Jackie has an inspiration. She attends college in the area of the property, and she knows three girls who are willing to pay $500 each per month in rent. Furthermore, she could live there rent-free, an indirect savings to her parents.

Joe and Kate think that their problem is solved. Every month, in a timely manner, International Bank and Trust receives the three checks from the roommates in a single envelope, and every month IB&T credits each of Joe and Kate's IRAs with $750. Then one month, Jackie, trying to simplify matters, has the three roommates write their checks to her, and then sends her personal check for $1,500 to IB&T. No sooner does her check reach IB&T than the bank is on the phone to Joe and Kate asking about it. Joe and Kate explain that their daughter Jackie isn't paying rent to live there; only the three roommates are. They thought that because she wasn't paying anything, it didn't matter that she lived there.

Unfortunately for Joe and Kate and their IRAs, the transaction is prohibited. Jackie is a disqualified person and cannot receive any benefit from her parents' IRAs—including free rent!

Mixing Business with Pleasure

Steve and Susan really like the income potential of a condo in Maui. They find a timeshare condo in Wailea available for $200,000, with an estimated annual income of $25,000 from vacationers, and strong indicators that the unit's value will appreciate annually. After the purchase, they can lease it out through a servicing company in Lahaina.

Susan has $250,000 in a traditional IRA that she had rolled over from a large 401(k) with her previous employer. Before purchasing the timeshare condo, she decides to convert the traditional IRA to a Roth IRA. With losses carried forward from previous years and the couple's mortgage interest deduction, the tax on the conversion is $30,000, which Susan and Steve pay partially from a home equity line on one of their rentals and partially from personal funds. Now the investment income from the $200,000 purchase using Susan's Roth funds will be tax-free forever, as will any investment income from the remaining $50,000. At Susan's direction, the Entrust Group perfects the security interest of the condo in Susan's IRA.

Susan and Steve like Wailea more than just for investing. They decide to spend their fall vacation at the condo/timeshare and make their reservation through the leasing agent. The agent sends the reservation to Entrust. Irene from Entrust is on the phone immediately. She tells Susan that the reservation *must* be canceled: Using their condo, even on a timeshare basis, is prohibited. If Susan and Steve stay there, Susan could lose her entire Roth, plus tax and penalties! However, Irene is also quick to lift Susan's audibly sagging spirits: Susan and Steve can rent any other unit in the same condo complex, as long as neither she nor any other disqualified person owns or has an interest in it. It may not be quite the same as staying in the place they own, but it wouldn't be illegal and wouldn't inflict a huge loss on Susan's IRA.

Susan and Steve have a good time on their vacation in the condo complex. And they feel that much better when they discover that a nice couple from Minnesota is renting their condo for a month!

A Financial Safety Tip for Hunters

Terry and Ben are both avid hunters. They decide to invest funds from their individual 401(k) plans in a hunting lease in northern South Dakota, which they, in turn, will sublease to other hunters. They also are permitted to build a small hunting lodge on the lease property.

Taking advantage of the Roth 401(k) deferrals in each of their accounts, Terry and Ben direct the trustees of their plans to fund the purchasing of the lease and the construction of the small lodge, each contributing $20,000 in Roth cash. The trustees execute the purchase through the Entrust Group, which is the third-party record keeper for the plans. Entrust perfects the lease and building in the name of "Duckblind LLC 401(k) Plan for the Benefit of Terry and Ben's Roth 401(k) Accounts." Both men are happy not to have had to do the paperwork on this one.

On their way to a hunting lease held by a friend of theirs in southern North Dakota, they decide to stop by their own lease and work on the lease and lodge now owned by their individual 401(k) accounts. First, they pick up their friend, Gordy, who's heading in the same direction to meet up with Keith, hunters all. But it also turns out that Gordy and Keith are pension consultants, a welcome stroke of luck for Ben and Terry. Gordy tells them that since they are disqualified persons, they can't work on their lease or the lodge, nor can they hunt on the property. When they get to their lease, Keith is already there. It's the very lease he and Gordy have rented! Keith agrees with Gordy—although it would have been a great hunting party for the four of them, Ben and Terry must bypass their lease and head up to their original destination in North Dakota.

The Wrong Way to a (Future) Mother-in-Law's Good Side

Frank's girlfriend, Edie, tells him that her mother wants to live near her grandchildren but can't afford to buy the townhouse that's for sale in the area. Frank, hoping to become engaged to Edie, decides to play the Good Samaritan and find a way for Harriet, Edie's mom, to make the purchase.

Frank wants to use his IRA to buy the townhouse, but he doesn't have enough money in it to cover the $152,000 purchase price. Edie, however, can make up the difference and then some. She can lend Frank's IRA $100,000 on an unsecured basis at 6 percent simple interest for 15 years. Then Harriet would rent the townhouse at a rate that would cover the loan owed by Frank's IRA to Edie plus condo fees, taxes, and insurance. Frank instructs his IRA administrator to purchase the property for all cash. Additionally, he has his IRA execute a rental agreement with Harriet.

In this case, the issues involved are not particularly clear. Frank's IRA received funds from his girlfriend, which permitted the IRA to buy a townhouse so that her mother could live in it. His IRA received a nonrecourse loan, and a nondisqualified person received the benefit of the townhouse. His IRA did not receive any disqualified funds because Edie is not his spouse. A question remains, though: What happens if Edie and Frank marry, and Harriet becomes Frank's mother-in-law? Then the transaction in fact may be prohibited.

A Change in Vacation Plans

Your individual 401(k) plan purchases a condo in the mountains of Colorado. The plan then proceeds to rent the condo out for $1,200 a month. With family vacationers in summer, hunters in fall, and skiers in winter, the condo has a steady stream of occupants except for the month of May. Considering how often the condo is in use, May would be a good time for minor repairs, painting, and cleanup. But you must not stay in the condo nor do the maintenance. Take your vacation anywhere you like, except at an asset owned by your plan or IRA, and find someone else to do the repair work.

How Close Is Too Close?

In some cases, the prohibited transaction rules set forth in IRS Code Section 4975 appear intentionally broad and cryptic. Frequently, we look to tax court decisions, private-letter rulings, and the pondering of experts to guide us to find the best investment offering while still steering clear of prohibited transaction pitfalls. The 2004 court case of *Joseph R. Rollins v. The Tax Commissioner* offers self-directed investors some clarification with regard to the prohibited transactions and further clarification of the definition of *disqualified persons*. The *Rollins* decision was based on the following set of circumstances: Rollins was the administrator for his own 401(k) plan. He also owned less than a controlling interest in three legal entities. Each of these entities borrowed money and executed a promissory note with Rollins's retirement plan at terms that would be considered fair market. Mr. Rollins acted as treasurer for these entities and was the signer on the promissory notes on behalf of the entities, as well as directing the plan to fund the loans.

In most cases, a disqualified person includes the IRA holder, lineal ascendants and descendants of the IRA holder, and any entity where the aggregate ownership share of disqualified persons constitutes a controlling interest. For example, if the son and daughter of an IRA holder owned 50 percent of Widgets 'R' Us LLC, the IRA could not do business with Widgets 'R' Us LLC, regardless of the fairness of the terms of the transaction. Using these rules, it seemed permissible for Mr. Rollins's plan to loan money to entities that were not disqualified because he did not own 50 percent of any of them.

While the definition of disqualified persons covers employers, employee organizations, such as collective-bargaining units, and other employer and family relationships, it is usually the IRA holder and his or her family members who are most often involved when deals are put together. The IRS has provided definitions of when transactions with these individuals run afoul of the prohibited transaction rules. As a result, transactions often are designed with those definitions in mind in order to avoid a prohibited transaction. Mr. Rollins did exactly that in designing the plan loans. He acknowledged that he personally was disqualified but that the transactions were with entities that were not. Yet the court decided that the loans gave him an indirect personal benefit and thus were prohibited transactions.

The *Rollins* decision caught some people off guard because of the "controlling interest" definition that has been used for so long. The resulting refinement of this definition has taught investors to look further into the structure of a transaction and examine who is negotiating for each entity, who is responsible for carrying out the terms of the agreement or note, and under which circumstances could the "use of" or "investment of" plan assets indirectly (or directly) benefit the interest of a disqualified person.

Rollins, the petitioner, owned from 9 to 33 percent interest in the three entities involved. Although he did not hold a controlling interest of 50 percent or greater, the judge made the following observations after ruling against Rollins:

- The petitioner was the single largest shareholder by a significant margin in all three entities. The comparison between his share and the shares of other shareholders was a focus of this decision.
- The petitioner held the positions of president, secretary, and treasurer, as well as being the registered agent of all the entities.
- The treasurer, Rollins, was the signer on all the notes securing the indebtedness.
- The notes were at higher than market value, and there was no default. Mr. Rollins's plan benefited from the security and the income of the investment.
- The court noted that Mr. Rollins had the burden of proving that he did not use the plan assets for his own benefit. The court determined that Mr. Rollins failed to carry this burden, noting specifically the sparse evidence presented.

It is clear from this case that the substance of the transaction, that is, "Was it a good or a bad investment?" had no bearing on the ruling against Rollins. Simplistically defining *controlling interest* as a percentage owned by a disqualified person was not looking deep enough into the issue of whether or not there is self-dealing in the transaction. Having disqualified persons involved in a transaction who are deemed to be receiving an indirect personal benefit, or *self-dealing*, results in the transaction being a prohibited transaction.

Self-directed plan investors structuring investments where disqualified persons or entities are involved, even in a less than controlling status, should realize that the IRS tax commissioner can, and obviously will, look deeper than the broad percentage guidelines. The commissioner will look for, among other things, convincing evidence that there is no personal benefit derived from the transaction, directly or indirectly, by those disqualified. Furthermore, investors must recognize that decisions with regard to prohibited transactions will not be decided solely on the merits of the investment itself. Prohibited transactions are just that—prohibited. As stated by the judge, "Good intentions and a pure heart are no defense."

Transactions to Avoid

There are specific real estate transactions that could jeopardize your retirement fund or create a taxable event, such as borrowing money from it, selling property to it, using it as a security for a loan, or buying property for present or future personal use.

Big Al's Bad Deal

"Big Al" has a great investment property in a major city that he purchased several years ago for $20,000 and that has appreciated considerably. He also has Roth IRA funds that he wants to put to work for him. He knows that he can't direct his Roth IRA to buy the investment property from him, at least not without a prohibited transaction exemption. And he figures that his chances of getting such an exemption from the Department of Labor are slim to none.

Al has a proposition for his good friend, Mark: Al will sell the property to Mark for $20,000 and pay Mark an additional $2,000 for helping him out. The title company will record the property transaction with Mark as the buyer, whereas Al as the seller will pay all title insurance, document fees, and transfer taxes. Mark agrees, and the deal is done.

On recording of the sale, Al directs his IRA administrator to buy the property from Mark for $25,000. The IRA administrator, Carla, works with the title company to execute the purchase for Al. Meanwhile, Mark calls up Carla, telling her how he'd done the deal with Al and wanting to know more about how IRAs can buy and sell property—he'd never heard of such a thing before. Carla says that yes, he can buy and sell real estate with IRA or 401(k) funds. However, she also realizes that she needs to look more closely at the transaction between Al and Mark.

When Al learns of Mark's conversation with Carla, he knows that he's in trouble. As he suspected all along, the Department of Labor would not have granted him a prohibited transaction exemption. The property was not being sold at fair market value, there was a commission involved, and it certainly did not qualify as an arm's-length transaction. At the very least, Al was violating the "indirect" rule, which states, "That which can be done directly should not be done indirectly." Once Carla gets back to Mark and explains to him the problems with the transaction, he quitclaims the property back to Al. Al loses $5,000 because he tried to skirt the laws governing IRA funds.

None of this diminishes Mark's newfound interest in using self-directed IRAs for his real estate business. In fact, he and Al team up to do many successful property deals using their IRA and 401(k) funds, each time making extra sure that they play by the rules.

A Costly Lesson in the Kitchen

Jack instructs his IRA to buy a triplex, with the IRA borrowing 60 percent of the purchase price from a national nonrecourse lender. Jack is confident that he's made a smart move: The triplex is fully rented, and its net operating income is enough to cover the $6,250 mortgage payments plus insurance and real property taxes.

Only a month after the purchase, a fire starts in the kitchen of one of the units. The fire is contained, but not until smoke damage renders that unit and one of the other units uninhabitable. Jack's IRA promptly files an insurance claim, but the insurance company does not respond in time to meet the IRA's obligation to pay the $6,250 mortgage.

Jack is faced with a problem: His IRA has only $2,000 left in it. He decides to make the mortgage payment personally to prevent his IRA from being in arrears. However, this potentially means a prohibited transaction because Jack may be making an excess contribution to his IRA. Instead, he should have made his allowable $5,000 contribution to his IRA for the year and then instructed the IRA to make the mortgage payment.

The next month, things go much better for Jack. The insurance company pays the loss claims to his IRA, and his IRA doesn't have any additional out-of-pocket expenses. However, if Jack's IRA had suffered another month of insufficient cash, he would have needed to contribute to his IRA and claim those contributions as excess contributions, potentially subject to a 6 percent penalty annually, as well as perhaps constituting a prohibited transaction.

Jack has learned that it is always wise to have adequate cash or other liquid assets in his IRA in the event of unexpected kitchen fires and the like.

Widgets Aren't Worth It

You own 40 percent of the stock of Widgets, Inc., a C corporation, but do not serve in any other capacity with the company. The company is growing very rapidly and needs to expand its physical plant. Fortuitously, at least for Widgets, the owner of the building next door files for bankruptcy. The bankruptcy court puts the building up for sale at a price significantly below fair-market value. Widgets' cash flow is too tight to make the purchase, and it doesn't have the track record to borrow that much money from the bank. Thus you come up with a plan: Your IRA buys 75 percent of the building for cash, and Widgets buys the remaining 25 percent. Your IRA then leases its 75 percent interest to Widgets at fair-market rents. Further, it gives Widgets the option—for $10,000 in option consideration—to buy out the 75 percent within five years at the then-current fair-market value. This is a prohibited transaction. If the building is such a terrific deal when it's in bankruptcy court, take a distribution from your IRA, pay the tax, and buy the entire building yourself.

A Mixed Diagnosis for Dr. Jeff

Dr. Jeff has a growing medical practice. He decides to close out his defined-benefit plan and convert it to a defined-contribution plan to cover himself and his employees.

Dr. Jeff opens a self-directed 401(k) plan at International Bank and Trust. On filing the final tax reports, he rolls his defined-benefit plan balance of $2.5 million into the 401(k). He opts for an audited annual financial statement for the plan to keep everything clean and above board.

The good doctor hires an administrator to take care of plan needs for himself and his employees. It's a great plan. Some of the options he's offering his employees include the ability to borrow up to 50 percent of their account balance, in-service withdrawals after two years, and be 100 percent vested when they are eligible for all contributions made by Dr. Jeff. As an added bonus, they can even roll their old 401(k) plan funds and IRAs to Dr. Jeff's plan if they wish. In all respects, this is a very flexible plan with most of the options that an employee would want.

Now that the plan is up and running, Dr. Jeff has another idea. He wants to purchase an office building in a strip center that includes a fitness center with some of his $2.5 million and use it as an income property. He directs himself in writing, in his capacity as trustee of his plan, to buy the office building for $3 million. His local banker will lend him $1.5 million on a nonrecourse basis, with his 401(k) to fund the other $1.5 million. The building will be owned beneficially by his 401(k) plan, with Dr. Jeff as trustee, for the benefit of Dr. Jeff.

Dr. Jeff has yet another idea. He will move his medical practice into the building, as well as retaining current tenants, one of which is his wife Juanita's foreign-exchange business. And then all his employees could exercise during their lunch break. While Dr. Jeff busies himself with the lease agreements and the details of his future office space, his attorney, Chuck, realizes that the owner of the building is going to be Dr. Jeff's 401(k). Chuck breaks the news to Dr. Jeff: He can't move his practice into the building. And it gets worse: Juanita has to move her business out of the building before the closing because her continued use of the property owned by her husband's 401(k) would constitute a prohibited transaction.

At least Chuck has *some* good news for Dr. Jeff. The doctor's plan administrator can use a portion of the building for plan administration business. Also, because the debt involved in the acquisition of the building is for his qualified plan, it would not be subject to unrelated debt-financed income tax, meaning more profit for him. So, although Dr. Jeff won't be shedding pounds during his lunch-time workouts, his 401(k) will be gaining.

Exemptions

The Department of Labor (DOL) has the authority to grant prohibited transaction exemptions. Individual exemptions apply only to the entity that obtains it, and class exemptions apply on an industry-wide basis. Table 9-1 lists some helpful Web sites regarding exemptions and the DOL.

TABLE 9-1 Web Sites Regarding Exemptions and the DOL

Listing of all class exemptions	www.dol.gov/ebsa/Regs/ClassExemptions/main.html
Information on obtaining an individual exemption	www.dol.gov/ebsa/regs/ind_exemptionsmain.html
EXPRO exemptions (special class of expedited individual exemptions)	www.dol.gov/ebsa/Regs/expro_exemptions.html
Advisory opinion whether a transaction would violate the prohibited transaction rules (do not ask for an opinion if you are not willing to accept the answer)	www.dol.gov/ebsa/Regs/AOs/main.html
Answers to inquiries regarding DOL regulations	www.dol.gov/ebsa/regs/ils/main.html

Correcting Prohibited Transactions

If you participated in a prohibited transaction, you can minimize the tax by correcting it as soon as possible. Correcting it means undoing it as much as you can without putting the plan in a worse financial position than if you had acted under the highest fiduciary standards.

 If you do not correct the transaction during the taxable period, you are subject to a 100 percent tax on the amount involved. The amount is based on the highest fair-market value for the property during the taxable period. You usually have an additional 90 days after the postmark of the notice of deficiency mailed by the IRS to correct the transaction. You can request the IRS to extend the correction period (the taxable period plus the 90 days) for a reasonable amount of time to make the correction or petition the tax court. If you correct the transaction within the allotted time, the IRS will abate, credit, or refund the 100 percent tax.

10

Taking Distributions

When you are eligible to take distributions from your retirement account, you can opt to receive either the entire sum or periodic distributions for the rest of your life. You can start taking distributions at age 59½ (or earlier if you have a qualified plan that allows for retirement at age 55), even if you are still working. However, with the exception of a Roth IRA (and not including a Roth 401(k)), you must start taking distributions in the year that you are age 70½. Even Roth 401(k) funds must begin distribution after age 70½, but if you are still employed, you may continue to make deferrals to your Roth or other 401(k) account.

You can take in-kind distributions from self-direction plans and individual retirement accounts (IRAs). Partial real property distributions are taken as undivided interests. Partial note distributions are taken in partial notes as determined by the distribution schedule.

Taking Early Distributions

If you withdraw assets (money or property) before age 59½, you must pay a 10 percent penalty tax on the taxable distribution in addition to your regular income tax, unless you qualify for one of the following exceptions:

- To pay significant unreimbursed medical expenses
- To pay medical insurance premiums after losing your job
- Purchasing a first home
- Disability
- Death
- Divorce and separation

If you make a contribution to your retirement fund, take no deduction for it, and withdraw it and any earnings on it before the due date (including extensions) of your income tax return for that year, the 10 percent additional tax does not apply. However, any interest or other income earned on the contribution, which also must be withdrawn, is treated as income in the year the contribution was made. These earnings must be reported and might be subject to the 10 percent early-withdrawal tax.

Note that if you withdraw funds from a SIMPLE IRA within two years of beginning participation, you must pay a 25 percent tax.

Paying Unreimbursed Medical Expenses

You do not have to pay the 10 percent tax on amounts you withdraw that are not more than the amount you paid for unreimbursed medical expenses during the year of the withdrawal, minus 7.5 percent of your adjusted gross income for the year of the withdrawal.

Paying Medical Insurance

You might not have to pay the 10 percent tax on amounts you withdraw during the year that are not more than the amount you paid during the year for medical insurance for yourself, your spouse, and your dependents if all the following conditions apply:

- You lost your job.
- You received unemployment compensation paid under any federal or state law for 12 consecutive weeks.
- You make the withdrawals during either the year you received the unemployment compensation or the following year.
- You make the withdrawals no later than 60 days after you have been reemployed.

Purchasing a First Home

You can withdraw $10,000 from your retirement fund for a first home without paying the 10 percent early-withdrawal tax. You must use the distribution to buy, build, or rebuild a first home that is the principal residence of yourself, your spouse, your child or grandchild, your spouse's child or grandchild, or a parent or other ancestor of your or your spouse.

Disability

If you become disabled, any amounts you withdraw from your IRA because of your disability are not subject to the 10 percent additional tax. You must furnish proof that you cannot do any substantial gainful activity because of your physical or mental condition. A physician must determine that your condition is expected to result in death or to last a long and indefinite time.

Death

If you die before age 59½, the assets in your IRA can be distributed to your beneficiary or estate without paying the 10 percent tax. (For more information, see the section "Distribution after Death" below.)

Divorce and Separation

The Internal Revenue Service (IRS) Code permits certain distributions relating to child support, alimony, or marital property resulting from divorce or legal separation actions. A qualified domestic relations order (QDRO) must be obtained from a court having jurisdiction over the divorce or separation proceedings in the case of a qualified plan. IRAs may be divided by court order. In both cases, division can be made in accordance with a prenuptial agreement.

If you are required to transfer all the assets in an IRA, you can just change the name on the IRA to your spouse or former spouse. If you need to transfer a portion of the funds, you can direct the trustee of the IRA to transfer the amount directly to the trustee of a new or an existing IRA set up in the name of your spouse or former spouse. If your spouse or former spouse is allowed to keep his or her portion of the IRA assets in your existing IRA, you can direct the trustee to transfer the assets you are permitted to keep directly to a new or existing IRA set up in your name. The name on the IRA containing your spouse's or former spouse's portion of the assets then would be changed to show his or her ownership.

If you receive a distribution from a qualified employer plan because of a divorce or similar proceedings, you may be able to roll over all or part of it into an IRA. To qualify, the distribution must be one that would have been an eligible rollover distribution if it had been made to an employee, and it must be made under a QDRO.

Lifetime Distributions before Age 59½

You can receive distributions from your retirement plan as a series of substantially equal payments over your life (or your life expectancy) or over the lives of you and your beneficiary (or your joint life expectancies) without paying the 10 percent tax, even if you receive such distributions before age 59½. To do this, you must use an IRS-approved distribution method, and you must take at least one distribution annually.

Two other IRS-approved distribution methods available are the amortization method and the annuity-factor method. These methods are more complex and require professional assistance. The payments must continue for at least five years or until you reach age 59½, whichever is longer. The five-year rule does not apply if the distribution method changes because of death or disability.

If the payments change before the end of the required period for any reason other than death or disability, you are subject to the 10 percent tax.

Required Distributions

When you reach age 70½, you are required to take distributions by April 1 of the following year, except for Roth IRAs. You do not need to take the entire amount at once, but you must take a required minimum distribution (RMD) at least annually over your life expectancy. The RMD for any year after your 70½ year must be made by December 31 of that year. The RMD can be calculated by dividing an account's year-end fair-market value by the distribution period determined by the IRS.

There are three commonly used life-expectancy charts that help retirement account holders figure mandatory distributions. Table 10-1 is the most commonly used one. It does not apply to beneficiaries of a deceased IRA owner or if the sole beneficiary of the IRA is the participant's spouse who is more than 10 years younger than the participant. Note that the distribution schedules show the minimum amount. You can take more!

If your spouse is your sole beneficiary and is more than 10 years younger than you, your life expectancy is based on your combined ages. If you have no beneficiary, or if your beneficiary is not your spouse, the minimum distribution incidental benefit (MDIB) table is used to determine the distribution period. The MDIB rules establish a uniform distribution period based on a joint life expectancy of you and someone exactly 10 years younger than you.

TABLE 10-1   Required Minimum Distributions

To calculate the year's minimum distribution amount, take the age of the retiree in the distribution year and find the corresponding distribution period. Then divide the value of the IRA by the distribution period to find the required minimum distribution.

Age of retiree	Distribution period (in years)	Age of retiree	Distribution period (in years)	Age of retiree	Distribution period (in years)
70	27.4	86	14.1	102	5.5
71	26.5	87	13.4	103	5.2
72	25.6	88	12.7	104	4.9
73	24.7	89	12	105	4.5
74	23.8	90	11.4	106	4.2
75	22.9	91	10.8	107	3.9
76	22	92	10.2	108	3.7
77	21.2	93	9.6	109	3.4
78	20.3	94	9.1	110	3.1
79	19.5	95	8.6	111	2.9
80	18.7	96	8.1	112	2.6
81	17.9	97	7.6	113	2.4
82	17.1	98	7.1	114	2.1
83	16.3	99	6.7	115 or older	1.9
84	15.5	100	6.3		
85	14.8	101	5.9		

If you do not withdraw funds as required, or if you withdraw an amount that is less than the RMD, you may have to pay a 50 percent excise tax on the amount not withdrawn. The IRS may waive the penalty if you can show that it was due to a reasonable error and that appropriate steps have been or are being taken to remedy the shortfall.

If you have more than one IRA, you must determine the RMD separately for each IRA. However, you can total these minimum amounts and take the total RMD from just one IRA or several.

All retirement plan distributions of nonresidents (including former residents) are not subject to state taxation.

If you choose to take distributions over your lifetime, you can either purchase an annuity or leave the balance in the plan and receive minimum distributions on an annual basis.

Annuity Method

To meet the minimum distribution requirements, the annuity can be either a life annuity (with or without a term certain) or a term-certain annuity. A term-certain annuity covers a specific number of years. If the annuity has a term certain, the term certain cannot exceed your life expectancy. Once payments have commenced, the time period cannot be extended, even if the initial term certain was shorter than the period permitted under the regulations.

The amount that you must receive on or before your required beginning date (RBD) depends on the type of annuity you select. If the annuity is a life annuity or a life annuity with a term certain of less than 20 years, the initial distribution must be equivalent to one payment interval (e.g., monthly or quarterly). If the annuity is a term-certain annuity without a life contingency or a life annuity with a term certain exceeding 20 years, you must receive the equivalent of a year's worth of annuity payments on or before your RBD.

Annual Basis

One of the benefits of using the annual-basis method rather than an annuity is that you can take an amount greater than your RMD; however, you can never take less. With the annual-basis method, you calculate the RMD by dividing your plan's preceding year-end balance by your life expectancy:

RMD = prior year-end balance/applicable life expectancy

The year-end balance is the amount in the account as of December 31, increased by any contributions made after the close of the year but intended as a contribution for the preceding year and decreased by any distributions made after the close of the year to meet RMD requirements for the first distribution year.

Once the applicable life expectancy figure is determined in your seventieth year, it must be adjusted annually either using a recalculation or a nonrecalculation method.

Recalculation

If you are using the recalculation method, the applicable life expectancy is recalculated on an annual basis using the IRS life expectancy tables. If your applicable life expectancy is based on the combined ages of you and your spouse and one of you dies, that life expectancy is reduced to zero in the year following the death, and any subsequent RMD calculations are based on the single life expectancy of the surviving individual.

Nonrecalculation

If you are using the nonrecalculation method, the applicable life expectancy is determined in the year that you are 70½ and then reduced by one for each subsequent year. Death does not affect the nonrecalculated life expectancy figure.

Roth IRA Distributions

You are not required to take distributions from your Roth IRA at any age. Qualified distributions are not included in your gross income. A qualified distribution is any payment or distribution made after age 59½ or, if before age 59½, for the hardship exceptions described earlier.

Distributions are taxable if they are made within five tax years of when you first contributed to your Roth IRA or if you rolled over funds into the Roth IRA from a retirement fund other than a Roth IRA.

Traditional IRA Distributions

Your distributions from your traditional IRA might be fully or partly taxable depending on whether your IRA includes nondeductible contributions. If you made only deductible contributions to your IRA, you have no basis in your IRA, which means that all distributions are taxed as part of your gross income. If you made nondeductible contributions to your IRA, you have a cost basis equal to the amount of those contributions. The nondeductible contributions are not taxed when they are distributed to you because they are a return of your investment in your IRA.

If your IRA contains both deductible and nondeductible contributions, your distributions consist of a nontaxable portion (your basis) and a taxable portion (deducted contributions, earnings, and gains). Until you run out of basis, each distribution is partly taxable and partly nontaxable.

If you have a loss on your IRA investment, you can include it on your income tax return after all the amounts in all your IRA accounts have been distributed to you and the total distributions are less than your unrecovered basis. You claim the loss as a miscellaneous itemized deduction subject to the 2 percent limit.

401(k) Plan Distributions

Generally, a distribution cannot be made until the employee retires, dies, becomes disabled, or separates from service. A distribution may be made if the plan ends and no other defined-contribution plan is established or continued.

Distributions minus the prorated part of any cost basis are subject to income tax in the year they are distributed. Since most recipients have no cost basis, a distribution generally is fully taxable, unless it is rolled over into another retirement fund.

Qualified Plan Distributions

A plan must provide that each participant receives either the entire sum or regular lifetime periodic distributions by the required beginning date. Regular periodic distributions must meet the MDIB rules, as described earlier. The minimum distribution rules apply individually to each qualified plan. You cannot satisfy the requirement for one plan by taking a distribution from another.

Distributions from a qualified plan are included in your gross income for the taxable year in which the distribution is made. You can roll over distributions, unless they are required distributions or one in a series of equal periodic payments made over a single or joint life expectancy for a specified period of 10 or more years. Rolling over an eligible distribution into an IRA or another qualified plan is a way to defer the tax owed on the distribution.

If you receive a lump-sum distribution, you can use income averaging to lower your taxes. With income averaging, you still must pay tax on the distribution in the tax year in which the funds are distributed, but income averaging generally yields lower taxes because the amount of tax due is determined as if you had received the distribution in even amounts over a five-year period. If you use income averaging, you must file IRS Form 4972, Tax on Lump Sum Distributions.

If you receive a lump sum and choose to either income average or pay the capital gains, you cannot roll over any portion of the lump-sum distribution. Conversely, if you receive a lump-sum distribution and roll over a portion, you cannot use income averaging or capital gains tax options on the remaining amount.

The IRS periodically publishes annuity tables that permit recapturing taxes paid on contributions to be accounted for in annuity distributions. The annuity provider should provide you with the appropriate calculations.

Distribution after Death

Your beneficiaries can be your spouse, estate, dependents, or anyone you choose to receive the benefits of your retirement fund after you die. The designated beneficiary is determined at of the end of the year following the year of the owner's death. If there is more than one beneficiary, the designated beneficiary is the one with the shortest life expectancy. The beneficiaries of your IRA must include the distributions to them in their gross incomes.

The designated beneficiary can receive payments over the beneficiary's life expectancy, regardless of whether the owner of the fund died before or after the RBD. The beneficiary's life expectancy is calculated using his or her age in the year following the owner's death and is reduced by one in each succeeding year.

If the owner does not have a designated beneficiary, the remaining payments must be made over the life expectancy of the owner, determined by the owner's age in the year of death and reduced by one each succeeding year.

If you inherit an IRA from your spouse, you can elect to treat it as your own after the RMD for the year of your spouse's death is distributed, as long as you are the sole beneficiary. Any distribution you take before you reach age 59½ may be subject to the 10 percent tax.

A surviving spouse can roll over part or all of any eligible rollover distribution received from an employer's qualified plan into an IRA but not into another qualified employer plan or annuity.

If you inherit an IRA from someone other than your spouse, you cannot treat it as though you established it. You cannot roll the funds into another IRA, nor can you contribute or roll funds into the inherited IRA. Deductions for amounts paid into the inherited IRA are not allowed, nor can nondeductible contributions be made to an inherited IRA.

Inheriting an IRA with Basis

If you inherit an IRA with basis, that basis must remain with the IRA. Unless you are the deceased's spouse and choose to treat the IRA as your own, you cannot combine the basis with any basis you have in your own IRAs or any basis in IRAs you inherited from other people. If you take a distribution from an inherited IRA as well as your own, and each has basis, you must complete Form 8606 for each IRA to determine the taxable and nontaxable portions of the distributions.

Deducting Federal Estate Tax

As a beneficiary, you might be able to deduct the estate tax paid on any part of a distribution that you must include as income from an inherited IRA. You can take the deduction for the tax year in which you report that income.

Any taxable part of a distribution that is not income in respect of a decedent is a payment that you must include in income. However, you cannot take any estate tax deduction for this part.

Rollovers

If your distribution from an employer plan is more than $200 for the year, you must be given the option to have any part of an eligible rollover distribution paid directly to an IRA or to an eligible retirement plan. If you do a direct rollover, no tax is withheld. Involuntary cash-outs between $1,000 and $5,000 are automatically rolled into an IRA selected by the plan administrator if you do not specify how to distribute the assets.

If you receive property and cash in an eligible rollover distribution from your employer's plan, you can roll over either the property or the cash or any combination of the two.

Contributing cash representing the fair-market value of property received in a distribution from a qualified retirement plan to an IRA does not qualify as a rollover if you keep the property. You must either roll over the property or sell it and roll over the proceeds. You cannot substitute your own funds for property you receive from your employer's retirement plan.

If you sell the distributed property and roll over all the proceeds into an IRA, no gain or loss is recognized. The sale proceeds (including any increase in value) are treated as part of the distribution and are not included in your gross income. You cannot roll over a life insurance contract from a qualified plan into an IRA.

Section 4975, Tax on Prohibited Transactions

Sec. 4975. Tax on Prohibited Transactions

(a) Initial Taxes on Disqualified Person

There is hereby imposed a tax on each prohibited transaction. The rate of tax shall be equal to15 percent of the amount involved with respect to the prohibited transaction for each year (or part thereof) in the taxable period. The tax imposed by this subsection shall be paid by any disqualified person who participates in the prohibited transaction (other than a fiduciary acting only as such).

(b) Additional Taxes on Disqualified Person

In any case in which an initial tax is imposed by subsection (a) on a prohibited transaction and the transaction is not corrected within the taxable period, there is hereby imposed a tax equal to 100 percent of the amount involved. The tax imposed by this subsection shall be paid by any disqualified person who participated in the prohibited transaction (other than a fiduciary acting only as such).

(c) Prohibited Transaction

4975(c)(1) General Rule

For purposes of this section, the term "prohibited transaction" means any direct or indirect—

4975(c)(1)(A) sale or exchange, or leasing, of any property between a plan and a disqualified person;

4975(c)(1)(B) lending of money or other extension of credit between a plan and a disqualified person;

4975(c)(1)(C) furnishing of goods, services, or facilities between a plan and a disqualified person;

4975(c)(1)(D) transfer to, or use by or for the benefit of, a disqualified person of the income or assets of a plan;

4975(c)(1)(E) act by a disqualified person who is a fiduciary whereby he deals with the income or assets of a plan in his own interests or for his own account; or

4975(c)(1)(F) receipt of any consideration for his own personal account by any disqualified person who is a fiduciary from any party dealing with the plan in connection with a transaction involving the income or assets of the plan.

4975(c)(2) Special Exemption

The Secretary shall establish an exemption procedure for purposes of this subsection. Pursuant to such procedure, he may grant a conditional or unconditional exemption of any disqualified person or transaction, orders of disqualified persons or transactions, from all or part of the restrictions imposed by paragraph (1) of this subsection. Action under this subparagraph may be taken only after consultation and coordination with the Secretary of Labor. The Secretary may not grant an exemption under this paragraph unless he finds that such exemption is—

4975(c)(2)(A) administratively feasible,

4975(c)(2)(B) in the interests of the plan and of its participants and beneficiaries, and

4975(c)(2)(C) protective of the rights of participants and beneficiaries of the plan.

Before granting an exemption under this paragraph, the Secretary shall require adequate notice to be given to interested persons and shall publish notice in the Federal Register of the pendency of such exemption and shall afford interested persons an opportunity to present views. No exemption may be granted under this paragraph with respect to a transaction described in subparagraph (E) or (F) of paragraph (1) unless the Secretary affords an opportunity for a hearing and makes a determination on the record with respect to the findings required under subparagraphs (A), (B), and (C) of this paragraph, except that in lieu of such hearing the Secretary may accept any record made by the Secretary of Labor with respect to an application for exemption under section 408(a) of title I of the Employee Retirement Income Security Act of 1974.

4975(c)(3) Special Rule for Individual Retirement Accounts

An individual for whose benefit an individual retirement account is established and his beneficiaries shall be exempt from the tax imposed by this section with respect to any transaction concerning such account (which would otherwise be taxable under this section) if, with respect to such transaction, the account ceases to be an individual retirement account by reason of the application of section 408(e)(2)(A) or if section 408(e)(4) applies to such account.

4975(c)(4) Special Rule for Medical Savings Accounts

An individual for whose benefit a medical savings account (within the meaning of section 220(d)) is established shall be exempt from the tax imposed by this section with respect to any transaction concerning such account (which would otherwise be taxable under this section)if section 220(e)(2) applies to such transaction.

4975(c)(5) Special Rule for Education Individual Retirement Accounts

An individual for whose benefit an education individual retirement account is established and any contributor to such account shall be exempt from the tax imposed by this section with respect to any transaction concerning such account (which would otherwise be taxable under this section) if section 530(d) applies with respect to such transaction.

(d) Exemptions

Except as provided in subsection (f)(6), the prohibitions provided in subsection (c) shall not apply to—

4975(d)(1) any loan made by the plan to a disqualified person who is a participant or beneficiary of the plan if such loan—

4975(d)(1)(A) is available to all such participants or beneficiaries on a reasonably equivalent basis,

4975(d)(1)(B) is not made available to highly compensated employees (within the meaning of section 414(q)) in an amount greater than the amount made available to other employees,

4975(d)(1)(C) is made in accordance with specific provisions regarding such loans set forth in the plan,

4975(d)(1)(D) bears a reasonable rate of interest, and

4975(d)(1)(E) is adequately secured;

4975(d)(2) any contract, or reasonable arrangement, made with a disqualified person for office space, or legal, accounting, or other services necessary for the establishment or operation of the plan, if no more than reasonable compensation is paid therefor;

4975(d)(3) any loan to an 1 leveraged employee stock ownership plan (as defined in subsection (e)(7)), if—

4975(d)(3)(A) such loan is primarily for the benefit of participants and beneficiaries of the plan, and

4975(d)(3)(B) such loan is at a reasonable rate of interest, and any collateral which is given to a disqualified person by the plan consists only of qualifying employer securities (as defined in subsection (e)(8));

4975(d)(4) the investment of all or part of a plan's assets in deposits which bear a reasonable interest rate in a bank or similar financial institution supervised by the United States or a State, if such bank or other institution is a fiduciary of such plan and if—

4975(d)(4)(A) the plan covers only employees of such bank or other institution and employees of affiliates of such bank or other institution, or

4975(d)(4)(B) such investment is expressly authorized by a provision of the plan or by a fiduciary (other than such bank or institution or affiliates thereof) who is expressly empowered by the plan to so instruct the trustee with respect to such investment;

4975(d)(5) any contract for life insurance, health insurance, or annuities with one or more insurers which are qualified to do business in a State if the plan pays no more than adequate consideration, and if each such insurer or insurers is—

4975(d)(5)(A) the employer maintaining the plan, or

4975(d)(5)(B) a disqualified person which is wholly owned (directly or indirectly) by the employer establishing the plan, or by any person which is a disqualified person with respect to the plan, but only if the total premiums and annuity considerations written by such insurers for life insurance, health insurance, or annuities for all plans (and their employers) with respect to which such insurers are disqualified persons (not including premiums or annuity considerations written by the employer maintaining the plan) do not exceed 5 percent of the total premiums and annuity considerations written for all lines of insurance in that year by such insurers (not including premiums or annuity considerations written by the employer maintaining the plan);

4975(d)(6) the provision of any ancillary service by a bank or similar financial institution supervised by the United States or a State, if such service is provided at not more than reasonable compensation, if such bank or other institution is a fiduciary of such plan, and if—

4975(d)(6)(A) such bank or similar financial institution has adopted adequate internal safeguards which assure that the provision of such ancillary service is consistent with sound banking and financial practice, as determined by Federal or State supervisory authority, and

4975(d)(6)(B) the extent to which such ancillary service is provided is subject to specific guidelines issued by such bank or similar financial institution (as determined by the Secretary after consultation with Federal and State supervisory authority), and under such guidelines the bank or similar financial institution does not provide such ancillary service—

4975(d)(6)(B)(i) in an excessive or unreasonable manner, and

4975(d)(6)(B)(ii) in a manner that would be inconsistent with the best interests of participants and beneficiaries of employee benefit plans;

4975(d)(7) the exercise of a privilege to convert securities, to the extent provided in regulations of the Secretary but only if the plan receives no less than adequate consideration pursuant to such conversion;

4975(d)(8) any transaction between a plan and a common or collective trust fund or pooled investment fund maintained by a disqualified person which is a bank or trust company supervised by a State or Federal agency or between a plan and a pooled investment fund of an insurance company qualified to do business in a State if—

4975(d)(8)(A) the transaction is a sale or purchase of an interest in the fund,

4975(d)(8)(B) the bank, trust company, or insurance company receives not more than a reasonable compensation, and

4975(d)(8)(C) such transaction is expressly permitted by the instrument under which the plan is maintained, or by a fiduciary (other than the bank, trust company, or insurance company, or an affiliate thereof) who has authority to manage and control the assets of the plan;

4975(d)(9) receipt by a disqualified person of any benefit to which he may be entitled as a participant or beneficiary in the plan, so long as the benefit is computed and paid on a basis which is consistent with the terms of the plan as applied to all other participants and beneficiaries;

4975(d)(10) receipt by a disqualified person of any reasonable compensation for services rendered, or for the reimbursement of expenses properly and actually incurred, in the performance of his duties with the plan, but no person so serving who already receives full-time pay from an employer or an association of employers, whose employees are participants in the plan or from an employee organization whose members are participants in such plan shall receive compensation from such fund, except for reimbursement of expenses properly and actually incurred;

4975(d)(11) service by a disqualified person as a fiduciary in addition to being an officer, employee, agent, or other representative of a disqualified person;

4975(d)(12) the making by a fiduciary of a distribution of the assets of the trust in accordance with the terms of the plan if such assets are distributed in the same manner as provided under section 4044 of title IV of the Employee Retirement Income Security Act of 1974 (relating to allocation of assets);

4975(d)(13) any transaction which is exempt from section 406 of such Act by reason of section 408(e) of such Act (or which would be so exempt if such section 406 applied to such transaction) or which is exempt from section 406 of such Act by reason of section 408(b)(12) of such Act;

4975(d)(14) any transaction required or permitted under part 1 of subtitle E of title IV or section 4223 of the Employee Retirement Income Security Act of

1974, but this paragraph shall not apply with respect to the application of subsection (c)(1) (E) or (F); or

4975(d)(15) a merger of multiemployer plans, or the transfer of assets or liabilities between multiemployer plans, determined by the Pension Benefit Guaranty Corporation to meet the requirements of section 4231 of such Act, but this paragraph shall not apply with respect to the application of subsection (c)(1) (E) or (F).

(e) Definitions

4975(e)(1) Plan

For purposes of this section, the term "plan" means—

4975(e)(1)(A) a trust described in section 401(a) which forms a part of a plan, or a plan described in section 403(a), which trust or plan is exempt from tax under section 501(a),

4975(e)(1)(B) an individual retirement account described in section 408(a),

4975(e)(1)(C) an individual retirement annuity described in section 408(b),

4975(e)(1)(D) a medical savings account described in section 220(d),

4975(e)(1)(E) an education individual retirement account described in section 530, or

4975(e)(1)(F) a trust, plan, account, or annuity which, at any time, has been determined by the Secretary to be described in any preceding subparagraph of this paragraph.

4975(e)(2) Disqualified Person

For purposes of this section, the term "disqualified person" means a person who is—

4975(e)(2)(A) a fiduciary;

4975(e)(2)(B) a person providing services to the plan;

4975(e)(2)(C) an employer any of whose employees are covered by the plan;

4975(e)(2)(D) an employee organization any of whose members are covered by the plan;

4975(e)(2)(E) an owner, direct or indirect, of 50 percent or more of—

4975(e)(2)(E)(i) the combined voting power of all classes of stock entitled to vote or the total value of shares of all classes of stock of a corporation,

4975(e)(2)(E)(ii) the capital interest or the profits interest of a partnership, or

4975(e)(2)(E)(iii) the beneficial interest of a trust or unincorporated enterprise, which is an employer or an employee organization described in subparagraph (C) or (D);

4975(e)(2)(F) a member of the family (as defined in paragraph (6)) of any individual described in subparagraph (A), (B), (C), or (E);

4975(e)(2)(G) a corporation, partnership, or trust or estate of which (or in which) 50 percent or more of—

4975(e)(2)(G)(i) the combined voting power of all classes of stock entitled to vote or the total value of shares of all classes of stock of such corporation,

4975(e)(2)(G)(ii) the capital interest or profits interest of such partnership, or

4975(e)(2)(G)(iii) the beneficial interest of such trust or estate, is owned directly or indirectly, or held by persons described in subparagraph (A), (B), (C), (D), or (E);

4975(e)(2)(H) an officer, director (or an individual having powers or responsibilities similar to those of officers or directors), a 10 percent or more shareholder, or a highly compensated employee (earning 10 percent or more of the yearly wages of an employer) of a person described in subparagraph (C), (D), (E), or (G); or

4975(e)(2)(I) a 10 percent or more (in capital or profits) partner or joint venturer of a person described in subparagraph (C), (D), (E), or (G).

The Secretary, after consultation and coordination with the Secretary of Labor or his delegate, may by regulation prescribe a percentage lower than 50 percent for subparagraphs (E) and (G) and lower than 10 percent for subparagraphs (H) and (I).

4975(e)(3) Fiduciary

For purposes of this section, the term "fiduciary" means any person who—

4975(e)(3)(A) exercises any discretionary authority or discretionary control respecting management of such plan or exercises any authority or control respecting management or disposition of its assets,

4975(e)(3)(B) renders investment advice for a fee or other compensation, direct or indirect, with respect to any moneys or other property of such plan, or has any authority or responsibility to do so, or

4975(e)(3)(C) has any discretionary authority or discretionary responsibility in the administration of such plan.

Such term includes any person designated under section 405(c)(1)(B) of the Employee Retirement Income Security Act of 1974.

4975(e)(4) Stockholdings

For purposes of paragraphs (2)(E)(i) and (G)(i) there shall be taken into account indirect stockholdings which would be taken into account under section 267(c), except that, for purposes of this paragraph, section 267(c)(4) shall be treated as providing that the members of the family of an individual are the members within the meaning of paragraph (6).

4975(e)(5) Partnerships; Trusts

For purposes of paragraphs (2)(E)(ii) and (iii), (G)(ii) and (iii), and (I) the ownership of profits or beneficial interests shall be determined in accordance with the rules for constructive ownership of stock provided in section 267(c) (other than paragraph (3) thereof), except that section 267(c)(4) shall be treated as providing that the members of the family of an individual are the members within the meaning of paragraph (6).

4975(e)(6) Member of Family

For purposes of paragraph (2)(F), the family of any individual shall include his spouse, ancestor, lineal descendant, and any spouse of a lineal descendant.

4975(e)(7) Employee Stock Ownership Plan

The term "employee stock ownership plan" means a defined contribution plan—

4975(e)(7)(A) which is a stock bonus plan which is qualified, or a stock bonus and a money purchase plan both of which are qualified under section 401(a), and which are designed to invest primarily in qualifying employer securities; and

4975(e)(7)(B) which is otherwise defined in regulations prescribed by the Secretary.

A plan shall not be treated as an employee stock ownership plan unless it meets the requirements of section 409(h), section 409(o), and, if applicable, section 409(n)and section 664(g) and, if the employer has a registration-type class of securities (as defined in section 409(e)(4)), it meets the requirements of section 409(e).

4975(e)(8) Qualifying Employer Security

The term "qualifying employer security" means any employer security within the meaning of section 409(l). If any moneys or other property of a plan are invested in shares of an investment company registered under the Investment Company Act of 1940, the investment shall not cause that investment company or that investment company's investment adviser or principal underwriter to be treated as a fiduciary or a disqualified person for purposes of this section, except when an investment company or its investment adviser or principal underwriter acts in connection with a plan covering employees of the investment company, its investment adviser, or its principal underwriter.

4975(e)(9) Section Made Applicable to Withdrawal Liability Payment Funds

For purposes of this section—

4975(e)(9)(A) In General

The term "plan" includes a trust described in section 501(c)(22).

4975(e)(9)(B) Disqualified Person

In the case of any trust to which this section applies by reason of subparagraph (A), the term "disqualified person" includes any person who is a disqualified person with respect to any plan to which such trust is permitted to make payments under section 4223 of the Employee Retirement Income Security Act of 1974.

4975(f) Other Definitions and Special Rules

For purposes of this section—

4975(f)(1) Joint and Several Liability

If more than one person is liable under subsection (a) or (b) with respect to any one prohibited transaction, all such persons shall be jointly and severally liable under such subsection with respect to such transaction.

4975(f)(2) Taxable Period

The term "taxable period" means, with respect to any prohibited transaction, the period beginning with the date on which the prohibited transaction occurs and ending on the earliest of—

4975(f)(2)(A) the date of mailing a notice of deficiency with respect to the tax imposed by subsection (a) under section 6212,

4975(f)(2)(B) the date on which the tax imposed by subsection (a) is assessed, or

4975(f)(2)(C) the date on which correction of the prohibited transaction is completed.

4975(f)(3) Sale Or Exchange; Encumbered Property

A transfer or real or personal property by a disqualified person to a plan shall be treated as a sale or exchange if the property is subject to a mortgage or similar lien which the plan assumes or if it is subject to a mortgage or similar lien which a disqualified person placed on the property within the 10-year period ending on the date of the transfer.

4975(f)(4) Amount Involved

The term "amount involved" means, with respect to a prohibited transaction, the greater of the amount of money and the fair market value of the other property given or the amount of money and the fair market value of the other property received; except that, in the case of services described in paragraphs (2) and (10) of subsection (d) the amount involved shall be only the excess compensation. For purposes of the preceding sentence, the fair market value—

4975(f)(4)(A) in the case of the tax imposed by subsection (a), shall be determined as of the date on which the prohibited transaction occurs; and

4975(f)(4)(B) in the case of the tax imposed by subsection (b), shall be the highest fair market value during the taxable period.

4975(f)(5) Correction

The terms "correction" and "correct" mean, with respect to a prohibited transaction, undoing the transaction to the extent possible, but in any case placing the plan in a financial position not worse than that in which it would be if the disqualified person were acting under the highest fiduciary standards.

4975(f)(6) Exemptions Not to Apply to Certain Transactions

4975(f)(6)(A) In General—

In the case of a trust described in section 401(a) which is part of a plan providing contributions or benefits for employees some or all of whom are owner-employees (as defined in section 401(c)(3)), the exemptions provided by subsection (d) (other than paragraphs (9) and (12)) shall not apply to a transaction in which the plan directly or indirectly—

4975(f)(6)(A)(i) lends any part of the corpus or income of the plan to,

4975(f)(6)(A)(ii) pays any compensation for personal services rendered to the plan to, or

4975(f)(6)(A)(iii) acquires for the plan any property from, or sells any property to, any such owner-employee, a member of the family (as defined in section 267(c)(4)) of any such owner-employee, or any corporation in which any such owner-employee owns, directly or indirectly, 50 percent or more of the total combined voting power of all classes of stock entitled to vote or 50 percent or more of the total value of shares of all classes of stock of the corporation.

4975(f)(6)(B) Special Rules for Shareholder-Employees, Etc.

4975(f)(6)(B)(i) In general—

For purposes of subparagraph (A), the following shall be treated as owner-employees:

4975(f)(6)(B)(i)(I) A shareholder-employee.

4975(f)(6)(B)(i)(II) A participant or beneficiary of an individual retirement plan (as defined in section 7701(a)(37)).

4975(f)(6)(B)(i)(III) An employer or association of employees which establishes such an individual retirement plan under section 408(c).

4975(f)(6)(B)(ii) Exception for Certain Transactions Involving Shareholder-Employees—

Subparagraph (A)(iii) shall not apply to a transaction which consists of a sale of employer securities to an employee stock ownership plan (as defined in subsection (e)(7)) by a shareholder-employee, a member of the family (as defined in section 267(c)(4)) of such shareholder-employee, or a corporation in which such a shareholder-employee owns stock representing a 50 percent or greater interest described in subparagraph (A).

4975(f)(6)(C) Shareholder-employee—

For purposes of subparagraph (B), the term 'shareholder-employee' means an employee or officer of an S corporation who owns (or is considered as owning within the meaning of section 318(a)(1)) more than 5 percent of the outstanding stock of the corporation on any day during the taxable year of such corporation.

4975(g) Application of Section

This section shall not apply—

4975(g)(1) in the case of a plan to which a guaranteed benefit policy (as defined in section 401(b)(2)(B) of the Employee Retirement Income Security Act of 1974) is issued, to any assets of the insurance company, insurance service, or insurance organization merely because of its issuance of such policy;

4975(g)(2) to a governmental plan (within the meaning of section 414(d)); or

4975(g)(3) to a church plan (within the meaning of section 414(e)) with respect to which the election provided by section 410(d) has not been made.

In the case of a plan which invests in any security issued by an investment company registered under the Investment Company Act of 1940, the assets of such plan shall be deemed to include such security but shall not, by reason of such investment, be deemed to include any assets of such company.

4975(h) Notification of Secretary Of Labor

Before sending a notice of deficiency with respect to the tax imposed by subsection (a) or (b), the Secretary shall notify the Secretary of Labor and provide him a reasonable opportunity to obtain a correction of the prohibited transaction or to comment on the imposition of such tax.

4975(i) Cross Reference

For provisions concerning coordination procedures between Secretary of Labor and Secretary of the Treasury with respect to application of tax imposed by this section and for authority to waive imposition of the tax imposed by subsection (b), see section 3003 of the Employee Retirement Income Security Act of 1974.

(Added Pub. L. 93-406, Title II, Sec. 2003(a), Sept. 2, 1974, 88 Stat. 971, and amended Pub. L. 94-455, Title XIX, Sec. 1906(b)(13)(A), Oct. 4, 1976, 90 Stat. 1834; Pub. L. 95-600, Title I, Sec. 141(f)(5), (6), Nov. 6, 1978, 92 Stat. 2795; Pub. L. 96-222, Title I, Sec. 101(a)(7)(C), (K), (L)(iv)(III), (v)(XI), Apr. 1, 1980, 94 Stat. 198-201; Pub. L. 96-364, Title II, Sec. 208(b), 209(b), Sept. 26, 1980, 94 Stat. 1289, 1290; Pub. L. 96-596, Sec. 2(a)(1)(K),(L), (2)(I), (3)(F), Dec. 24, 1980, 94 Stat. 3469, 3471; Pub. L. 97-448, Title III, Sec. 305(d)(5), Jan. 12, 1983, 96 Stat. 2400; Pub. L. 98-369, Div. A, Title IV, Sec. 491(d)(45), (46), (e)(7), (8), July 18, 1984, 98 Stat. 851-853; Pub. L. 99-514, Title XI, Sec. 1114(b)(15)(A), Title XVIII, Sec. 1854(f)(3)(A), 1899A(51), Oct. 22, 1986, 100 Stat. 2452, 2882, 2961; Pub. L. 101-508, Title XI, Sec. 11701(m), Nov. 5, 1990, 104 Stat. 1388-513; Pub. L. 104-188, Title I, Sec. 1453(a), 1702(g)(3), Aug. 20, 1996, 110 Stat. 1755; Pub. L. 104-191, Title III, Sec. 301(f), Aug. 21, 1996, 110 Stat. 1936 ; Pub. L. 105-34, Title II, X, XV, XVI, Sec. 213(b)(1), 213(b)(2), 1074(a), 1506(b)(1)(A), 1506(b)(1)(B), 1602(a)(5), Aug. 5, 1997, 111 Stat 788; Pub. L. 105-206, Title VI, Sec. 6023(19), July 22, 1998, 112 Stat 685.)

Figure A-1 is an example of an adoption agreement for a qualified plan.

ADOPTION AGREEMENT
PROTOTYPE EXPANDED PROFIT-SHARING
PLAN AND TRUST

The undersigned Employer hereby adopts the Sponsor's Prototype Expanded Profit-Sharing Plan in the form of a standardized Plan, as set out in this Adoption Agreement and the Prototype Defined Contribution Plan Document #01, and agrees that the following definitions, elections and terms shall be part of such Plan.

GENERAL INFORMATION

1(a) Name & Street Address of Employer:

(b) Employer ☐ is ☐ is not part of a Controlled Group or Affiliated Service Group. If "yes", complete Attachment A.

2. Phone:_____ 3. Trustee/Custodian:_____

4. Type of Business Entity: ☐ C Corporation, Date of incorporation _____; ☐ S Corporation, Date of incorporation _____;

☐ Partnership; ☐ Sole Proprietor; ☐ Other: _____

5. Employer's Taxable Year: _____

6. EIN #:_____ 7. 3-Digit Plan Number:_____ 8. Business Code:

9. Plan Administrator: ☐ a. Employer ☐ b. Other (Specify): _____

10. Sponsor: _____

    Address: _____ Phone:_____

11. Depository:_____

12. This is a: ☐ (a) new plan with an effective date of:

          ☐ (b) restatement of a plan previously adopted by the Employer with an effective date of:_____,
              and an initial effective
              date of:

          ☐ (c) amendment of a plan with an effective date of:_____ and an initial effective date of:

          ☐ (d) merger, amendment and restatement of the _____ and the
              into the

              _____. The effective date of the merger is:_____. The initial
              effective date of the surviving plan was _____.

          ☐ (e) restatement of the _____ effective _____, and a restatement of the _____ effective
              , and a merger of the
              _____ into the _____.

13. This Plan shall be governed by the laws of _____

14. Plan Year shall mean: ☐ calendar year; or ☐ the 12-consecutive month period beginning on_____; or ☐ an initial short Plan Year beginning on_____ and ending on_____ and thereafter the 12-consecutive month period beginning
    on _____ and ending on _____.

15. The Limitation Year shall mean: ☐ calendar year; or ☐ the 12-consecutive month period beginning on _____; or an initial short Limitation Year beginning on_____ and ending on_____ and thereafter the 12-consecutive month period beginning on
    _____ and ending on _____.

16. Valuation Date(s) is (are): ☐ Daily; ☐ The last day of the Plan Year; or ☐ The last day of the following months of the Plan Year: _____;
    ☐ Other: _____

17. Compensation shall mean all of each Participant's:

    (a) ☐ Form W-2 wages; or ☐ Section 3401(a) wages; or ☐ 415 safe-harbor compensation.

    (b) Compensation shall be determined over the following Determination period: ☐ the Plan Year; or ☐ a consecutive 12-month period ending with or within the Plan Year. Enter the day and the month this period begins: _____ (day) _____ (month). For Employees whose date of hire is less than 12 months before the end of the 12-month period designated, compensation will be determined over the Plan Year.

    (c) Compensation ☐ shall ☐ shall not include Employer contributions made pursuant to a salary reduction agreement which are not includible in gross income of the Employee under Sections 125, 132(f)(4), 402(e)(3), 402(h)(1)(B) or 403(b) of the Code.

    (d) For purposes of allocating Employer Contributions, Compensation ☐ shall ☐ shall not include amounts paid prior to a Participant's Entry Date.

FIGURE A-1   Adoption Agreement for a Qualfied Plan

18. (a) Early Retirement Age shall mean:
☐ Not applicable; ☐ Age _____ (not less than Age 55) and completion of _____ Years of Service.

   (b) Normal Retirement Age shall mean: ☐ Age____(not to exceed age 65); or ☐ the later of age____(not to exceed age 65) or the____(not to exceed 5th) anniversary of the Participation Commencement Date. If, for Plan Years beginning before January 1, 1988, Normal Retirement Age was determined with reference to the anniversary of the participation commencement date (more than 5 but not to exceed 10 years), the anniversary date for Participants who first commenced participation under the Plan before the first Plan Year beginning on or after January 1, 1988, shall be the earlier of (a) the tenth anniversary of the date the Participant commenced participation in the Plan (or such anniversary as had been elected by the Employer, if less than 10) or (b) the fifth anniversary of the first day of the first Plan Year beginning on or after January 1, 1988. The Participation Commencement Date is the first day of the first Plan Year in which the Participant commenced participation in the Plan.

   (c) Definition of Highly Compensated Employee:
   ☐ (1) In determining who is a Highly Compensated Employee the Employer makes a top paid group election. The effect of this election is that an Employee (who is not a 5-percent owner at any time during the determination year or the look-back year) with Compensation in excess of $80,000 (as adjusted) for the look-back year is a Highly Compensated Employee only if the Employee was in the top-paid group for the look-back year.
   ☐ (2) In determining who is a Highly Compensated Employee (other than as a 5-percent owner) the Employer makes a calendar year data election. The effect of this election is that the look-back year is the calendar year beginning with or within the look-back year.

ELIGIBILITY

19. All Employees of the Employer (including employers required to be aggregated under sections 414(b),(c), (m), or (o) of the Code) will be eligible to participate in this Plan except the following:
   ☐ (a) Employees who have not attained age____. (cannot exceed age 21).
   ☐ (b) Employees who have not completed____Year(s) of Service. (Cannot exceed 1 year unless the Plan provides a nonforfeitable right to 100% of the Participant's account balance derived from Employer contributions after not more than 2 years of service in which case up to 2 years is permissible. If the Year(s) of Service selected is or includes a fractional year, an employee will not be required to complete any specified number of Hours of Service to receive credit for such fractional year.)

20. All Employees who are members of eligible classes of employees shall be eligible to participate in the Plan except:
   ☐ (a) Employees included in a unit of Employees covered by a collective bargaining agreement as described in Section 14.07 of the Plan.
   ☐ (b) Employees who are nonresident aliens as described in Section 14.25 of the Plan.
   ☐ (c) Employees who become Employees as the result of a "§410(b)(6)(C) transaction". These Employees will be excluded during the period beginning on the date of the transaction and ending on the last day of the first Plan Year beginning after the date of the transaction. A "§410(b)(6)(C) transaction" is an asset or stock acquisition, merger, or similar transaction involving a change in the Employer of the Employees of a trade or business.

21. Eligibility under the Plan will be extended to all Employees who satisfied the eligibility requirements of this Plan with the following prior employer(s):

22. The eligibility and service requirements in Item #19 above ☐ are ☐ are not waived with respect to Employees employed on the Effective Date of this Plan. If these requirements are waived, such Employees shall become Participants in the Plan as of the Effective Date of the Plan.

SERVICE

23. Service for eligibility and vesting will be determined on the basis of the method selected below. Only one method may be selected and such method will be applied to all Employees covered under the Plan.
   ☐ (a) On the basis of actual hours for which an Employee is paid or entitled to payment.
   ☐ (b) On the basis of days worked. An Employee will be credited with ten (10) hours of service if under Section 14.21 of the Plan such Employee would be credited with at least one (1) Hour of Service during the day.
   ☐ (c) On the basis of weeks worked. An Employee will be credited with forty-five (45) Hours of Service if under Section 14.21 of the Plan such Employee would be credited with at least one (1) Hour of Service during the week.
   ☐ (d) On the basis of semi-monthly payroll periods. An Employee will be credited with ninety-five (95) Hours of Service if under Section 14.21 of the Plan such Employee would be credited with at least one (1) Hour of Service during the semi-monthly payroll period.
   ☐ (e) On the basis of months worked. An Employee will be credited with one hundred ninety (190) Hours of Service if under Section 14.21 of the Plan such Employee would be credited with at least one (1) Hour of Service during the month.
   ☐ (f) On the basis of Elapsed Time, as provided for in Section 14.37(b) of the Plan. (Do not complete Items 24 and 25).

24. A Year of Service shall mean a 12-consecutive month period during which an Employee completes at least (not to exceed 1000) Hours of Service with the Employer.

25. A Break in Service shall mean a 12-consecutive month period during which an Employee does not complete more than (not to exceed 500) Hours of Service.

FIGURE A-1   Adoption Agreement for a Qualfied Plan

26. Subsequent Eligibility Computation Periods under Section 2.02(a) shall commence with:
☐(a) the anniversary of the Employee's employment commencement date; or
☐(b) the Plan Year which commences prior to the Employee's first anniversary of his employment commencement date.

27. Subsequent Vesting Computation Periods under Section 5.03(b) shall commence with:
☐(a) the anniversary of the Employee's employment commencement date; or
☐(b) the Plan Year which commences prior to the Employee's first anniversary of his employment commencement date.

ENTRY DATE

28. An Employee who has completed the eligibility requirements shall enter the Plan on the following Entry Date:
☐ (a)   There are no age and service requirements. Entry Date shall mean the Employee's date of employment;
☐ (b)   The day on which the Employee satisfies the eligibility requirements.
☐ (c)   The first day of the Plan Year in which the Employee satisfies the eligibility requirements;
☐ (d)   The first day of the first month or the first day of the 7th month of the Plan Year coinciding with or next following the satisfaction of the Plan's eligibility requirements.
☐ (e)   The first day of the month in which the Participant satisfies the eligibility requirements
☐ (f)   The first day of the following month after the Employee satisfies the eligibility requirements;
☐ (g)   The first day of the Plan Year which immediately follows the Plan Year in which the Participant satisfies the eligibility requirements;
Note: Option (g) may not be selected unless the maximum age and service requirements selected under Items #19 and 51 are reduced by 1/2 year.
☐ (h)   The first day of each of the following months of the Plan Year (must include the 1st and the 7th month of the Plan Year):

29. Notwithstanding the Entry Date selected in Item 28 above, an Employee who has completed the eligibility requirements as of will (leave blank if inapplicable) will become a Participant immediately on such date, or the Entry Date specified in Item 28, if earlier.

NONELECTIVE EMPLOYER CONTRIBUTIONS

30. ☐   Employer Contributions will be allocated to each Participant in the ratio that such Participant's Compensation bears to the Compensation of all Participants. Note: If this Item is selected, Item 33 does not apply.

31. Employer contributions ☐ shall ☐ shall not be limited to the Employer's current or accumulated profits.

32. Employees who terminate employment during the Plan Year with not more than 500 hours of service and who are not Employees as of the last day of the Plan Year ☐ shall ☐shall not receive an allocation of Employer Contributions.

SOCIAL SECURITY INTEGRATION

33. The allocation of Employer Contributions and forfeitures ☐ shall ☐ shall not be integrated with Social Security.

34. If the allocation of Employer Contributions and forfeitures is integrated with Social Security complete the following:
(a)   The Integration Level will be:
☐(1) $_____ (may not exceed the Taxable Wage Base).
☐(2)   The Taxable Wage Base in effect on the first day of each Plan Year.
☐(3)   _____% of the Taxable Wage Base in effect on the first day of each Plan Year (may not exceed 100%).
(b)   The Excess Contribution Percentage (which may not exceed the Profit-Sharing Maximum Disparity Rate described in Section 3.04(e) of the Plan) will be
_____%

EMPLOYEE CONTRIBUTIONS

35. (a) Employee rollover contributions ☐ will ☐will, but only after becoming a Participant ☐ will not be permitted.
(b) Employee transfer contributions ☐ will☐ will, but only after becoming a Participant ☐ will not be permitted.
(c) Employee Nondeductible Contributions ☐ will ☐ will not be permitted.
(d) Employee Mandatory Contributions ☐ will ☐ will not be permitted.

VESTING AND FORFEITURE REQUIREMENTS

36. Each Participant's vested percentage in his Employer Contribution Account shall be determined as follows:
Note: The Employer may choose one Formula from (a), and must choose one from (b) below. Failure to make an election under (a) shall mean the election under (b) shall always apply.

FIGURE A-1   Adoption Agreement for a Qualfied Plan

(a) Non-Top-Heavy Vesting Formulas: The following Vesting Formula shall apply in years in which the Plan is not Top-Heavy.
- ☐ (1) Vesting Formula #1 - 100% vested after _____(not to exceed five) Years of Service.
- ☐ (2) Vesting Formula #2:

Years of Service	Vested Percentage
Less than 1	
1	
2	
3	_____(not less than 20%)
4	_____(not less than 40%)
5	_____(not less than 60%)
6	_____(not less than 80%)
7 or more	100%

☐ (3) The Top-Heavy Vesting Formula selected below shall apply at all times.

(b) Top-Heavy Vesting Formulas: The following Vesting Formula shall apply in years in which the Plan is Top-Heavy.
- ☐ (1) Vesting Formula #3 - 100% vested at all times
- ☐ (2) Vesting Formula #4 - 100% vested after_____(not to exceed three) Years of Service.
- ☐ (3) Vesting Formula #5:

Years of Service	Vested Percentage
Less than 1	
1	
2	_____(not less than 20%)
3	_____(not less than 40%)
4	_____(not less than 60%)
5	_____(not less than 80%)
6	100%

If the Vesting Formula under the Plans shifts in or out of the above Formula for any Plan Year because of the Plan's Top-Heavy status, such shift is an amendment of the Vesting Formula and the election in Section 12.03 of the Plan applies.

☐ (c) All Participants as of_____will be 100% vested as of the earlier of such date or the date specified by the Vesting Formula selected above.

37. (a) All of an Employee's Years of Service with the Employer are counted to determine the nonforfeitable percentage in the Employee's account balance
derived from Employer contributions except:
- ☐ (1) Years of Service before age 18;
- ☐ (2) Years of Service during a period for which the Employee made no mandatory contributions;
- ☐ (3) Years of Service before the Employer maintained this Plan or a predecessor plan;
- ☐ (4) Years of Service before January 1, 1971, unless the Employee has had at least 3 Years of Service after December 31, 1970;
- ☐ (5) Years of Service before the effective date of ERISA if such service would have been disregarded under the Break in Service rules of the prior plan in effect from time to time before such date. For these purposes, Break in Service rules are rules which result in the loss of prior vesting or benefit accruals, or which deny an employee eligibility to participate, by reason of separation or failure to complete a required period of service within a specified period of time.

(b) Years of Service for eligibility and vesting purposes will also include:
- ☐ (1) Years of Service with the following named predecessor employers:
- ☐ (2) Years of Service with the following named predecessor employers during the time a qualified plan was maintained:

38. Nonelective contribution forfeitures not used to restore Participant's Accounts will be (choose one):
- ☐ (a) allocated in addition to the Employer Contributions;
- ☐ (b) used to reduce otherwise required Employer contributions; or
- ☐ (c) used to reduce Employer Matching Contributions and any remainder allocated in addition to the Employer Contribution.

39. Forfeitures arising on account of distribution of a Participant's vested benefit, shall be allocated as of the last day of the Plan Year which is concurrent with or next follows:
- ☐ (a) Employee's termination of employment;
- ☐ (b) Employee having incurred a 1-year Break in Service;
- ☐ (c) Employee having incurred 2 consecutive 1-year Breaks in Service; or
- ☐ (d) Employee having incurred 5 consecutive 1-year Breaks in Service.

TOP-HEAVY PROVISIONS

40. Top-Heavy Status of Plan:
- ☐ (a) The Plan is deemed to be a Top-Heavy Plan and Article VIII shall apply at all times.

FIGURE A-1   Adoption Agreement for a Qualfied Plan

☐ (b) Article VIII shall apply only if the Plan is or becomes a Top-Heavy Plan.

41. Present Value: For purposes of establishing present value to compute the Top-Heavy Ratio, any benefit shall be discounted only for mortality and interest based on the following: Interest Rate:_____%   Mortality Table:
Valuation Date: For purposes of computing the top-heavy ratio the valuation date shall be _____ of each year.
☐ Not applicable, the Employer does not maintain a defined benefit plan.

42. If the Employer maintains another plan or plans covering any Participant under this Plan, the minimum allocation requirements applicable to Top-Heavy Plans:
☐ (a) will be met in this Plan.
☐ (b) will not be met in this Plan but will be net in the following plan or plans:

43. If any minimum allocation is required under Article VIII such allocations shall be made to the following Participants:
☐ All Participants; or ☐Only Non-Key Employees who are Participants.

OPTIONAL FORMS OF BENEFITS

44. The benefit options under the Plan include the following (check all options which apply):
☐ (a) Single sum payment;
☐ (b) Installment Payments over Single or Joint Life Expectancy;
☐ (c) Annuity Payments over the life or joint lives of the Participant and beneficiary;
   (d) If under the Plan a benefit will be paid in the form of a Joint and Survivor Annuity, the survivor annuity will be:
      ☐ 50%; ☐ 100%;
      ☐___% (not less than 50% and not greater than 100%) of the annuity payable during the joint lives of the Participant and Spouse.
If "(c)" is selected such annuity shall become the normal form of retirement benefit.

DISTRIBUTIONS

45. Unless earlier distribution is required by Sections 10.02 or 5.04 of the Plan, if a Participant terminates employment for a reason other than retirement on or after the Participant's Normal Retirement Age, death or Disability of the Participant, the Participant shall be eligible for payment of benefits as soon as administratively feasible following the:
☐ (a) last day of the Plan Year coincident with or next following the date of termination.
☐ (b) last day of Plan Year after the Participant incurs _____ (up to 5) consecutive 1-year Breaks in Service;
☐ (c) date of termination.

46.   (a) In-Service distributions ☐ are ☐ are not available.
   (b) The following in-service provisions apply to this Plan (check all that apply to this Plan and the contribution to which they apply):
      ☐ (1) The 24-month rule; ☐Nonelective; ☐ Matching; ☐ Employee Voluntary/Mandatory
      ☐ (2) The 60-month participation rule; ☐Nonelective; ☐ Matching; ☐ Employee Voluntary/Mandatory
      ☐ (3) Hardship distribution provisions; ☐Nonelective; ☐ Matching; ☐ Employee Voluntary/Mandatory
      ☐ (4) Financial Hardship Distribution Provisions. ☐Elective Deferrals; ☐other (List): _____
      ☐ (5) Attainment of Age _____ . ☐Elective Deferrals; ☐Nonelective; ☐ Matching; ☐ Employee Voluntary/Mandatory
      ☐ (6) Attainment of Age 59 1/2; ☐ Elective Deferrals
   (c) Rollover/Transfer contributions are available for distribution:
      ☐(1) at any time; or
      ☐(2) based on the nonelective distribution rules of the Plan.
   (d)   The Required Beginning Date of a Participant with respect to a Plan is (select one):
      ☐ (1) the April 1 of the calendar year following the calendar in which the Participant attains age 70½.
      ☐ (2) the April 1 of the calendar year following the calendar year in which the Participant attains age 70½ , except that benefit distributions to a Participant (other than a 5-percent owner) with respect to benefits accrued after the later of the adoption or effective date of the amendment to the Plan must commence by the later of the April 1 of the calendar year following the calendar year in which the Participant attains age 70½ or retires.
      ☐ (3) the later of the April 1 of the calendar year following the calendar year in which the Participant attains age 70½ or retires except that benefit distributions to a 5-percent owner must commence by the April 1 of the calendar year following the calendar year in which the Participant attains age 70½. (also select A, B, and/or C, whichever is applicable. (C) must be selected to the extent that there would otherwise be an elimination of a preretirement age 70½ distribution option for Employees older than those listed above.)
         ☐ (A) any Participant attaining age 70½ in years after 1995 may elect by April 1 of the calendar year following the year in which the Participant attained age 70½ , (or by December 31, 1997 in the case of a Participant attaining age 70½ in 1996) to defer distributions until the calendar year following the calendar year in which the Participant retires. If no such election is made the Participant will begin receiving distributions by the April 1 of the calendar year following the year in which the Participant attained age 70½ (or by December 31, 1997 in the case of a Participant attaining age 70½ in 1996)

FIGURE A-1   Adoption Agreement for a Qualfied Plan

□ (B) any Participant attaining age 70½ in years prior to 1997 may elect to stop distributions and recommence by the April 1 of the calendar year following the year in which the Participant retires. There is either (select one)

   □ (i) a new Annuity Starting Date upon recommencement, or
   □ (ii) no new Annuity Starting Date upon recommencement.

□ (C) the preretirement age 70½ distribution option is only eliminated with respect to employees who reach age 70½ in or after a calendar year that begins after the later of December 31, 1998, or the adoption date of the amendment. The preretirement age 70½ distribution option is an optional form of benefit under which benefits payable in a particular distribution form (including any modifications that may be elected after benefit commencement) commence at a time during the period that begins on or after January 1 of the calendar year in which an Employee attains age 70½ and ends April 1 of the immediately following calendar year.

LOAN PROVISIONS

47. Loans to Participants □ are □ are not available.

INSURANCE PROVISIONS

48. The Trustee □ shall □ shall not be authorized to purchase life insurance contracts on the lives of the Participants; and shall purchase such life insurance at the direction of the □ Plan Administrator □ the Participant.

INVESTMENT PROVISIONS

49. The Trustee shall invest in accordance with the provisions of the Trust Agreement attached hereto.

50. If elected below, the Trustee is authorized to invest an amount not to exceed the percentage of plan assets specified in qualified employer securities (as defined in section 407(d)(5) of ERISA).
   □ (a) Investment in qualified employer securities is not permitted.
   □ (b) Investment in qualified employer securities is permitted in an amount not to exceed _____% of plan assets.

CASH OR DEFERRED PLAN ELECTIONS

Note: The following CODA provisions shall apply: □ Traditional 401(k) (Article XV applies); □ Safe Harbor 401(k) (Article XVI applies); or □ SIMPLE 401(k) (Article XVII applies).

51.   Eligibility and Service Requirements:
   (a) Elective Deferrals:
      (1) Each Employee will be eligible to participate in this Plan in accordance with Section 15.01, except the following:
         □ (A) Employees who have not attained age____(cannot exceed age 21).
         □ (B) Employees who have not completed____Year(s) of Service. (Cannot exceed one year)
      (2) All Employees who are members of eligible classes of employees shall be eligible to participate in the Plan except:
         □ (A) Employees included in a unit of Employees covered by a collective bargaining agreement as described in Section 14.07 of the Plan.
         □ (B) Employees who are nonresident aliens as described in Section 14.25 of the Plan.
         □ (C) Employees who become Employees as the result of a "§410(b)(6)(C) transaction". These Employees will be excluded during the period beginning on the date of the transaction and ending on the last day of the first Plan Year beginning after the date of the transaction. A "§410(b)(6)(C) transaction" is an asset or stock acquisition, merger, or similar transaction involving a change in the Employer of the Employees of a trade or business.
      (3) The eligibility and service requirements outlined above □ are □ are not waived with respect to Employees employed on the Effective Date of this Plan. If these requirements are waived, such Employees shall become Participants in the Plan as of the Effective Date of the Plan.
   (b) Qualified Matching and Qualified Nonelective Contributions:
      (1) Each Employee will be eligible to participate in this Plan in accordance with Section 15.01, except the following:
         □ (A) Employees who have not attained age____(cannot exceed age 21).
         □ (B) Employees who have not completed____Year(s) of Service. (Cannot exceed two years)
      (2) All Employees who are members of eligible classes of employees shall be eligible to participate in the Plan except:
         □ (A) Employees included in a unit of Employees covered by a collective bargaining agreement as described in Section 14.07 of the Plan.
         □ (B) Employees who are nonresident aliens as described in Section 14.25 of the Plan.
         □ (C) Employees who become Employees as the result of a "§410(b)(6)(C) transaction". These Employees will be excluded during the period beginning on the date of the transaction and ending on the last day of the first Plan Year beginning after the date of the transaction. A "§410(b)(6)(C) transaction" is an asset or stock acquisition, merger, or similar transaction involving a change in the Employer of the Employees of a trade or business.
      (3) The eligibility and service requirements outlined above □ are □ are not waived with respect to Employees employed on the Effective Date of this Plan. If these requirements are waived, such Employees shall become Participants in the Plan as of the Effective Date of the Plan.
   (c) Matching Contributions:

FIGURE A-1   Adoption Agreement for a Qualfied Plan

(1)   Each Employee will be eligible to participate in this Plan in accordance with Section 15.01, except the following:
    ☐ (A) Employees who have not attained age____(cannot exceed age 21).
    ☐ (B) Employees who have not completed____Year(s) of Service. (Cannot exceed two years)
(2)   All Employees who are members of eligible classes of employees shall be eligible to participate in the Plan except:
    ☐ (A) Employees included in a unit of Employees covered by a collective bargaining agreement as described in Section 14.07 of the Plan.
    ☐ (B) Employees who are nonresident aliens as described in Section 14.25 of the Plan.
    ☐ (C) Employees who become Employees as the result of a "§410(b)(6)(C) transaction". These Employees will be excluded during the period beginning on the date of the transaction and ending on the last day of the first Plan Year beginning after the date of the transaction. A "§410(b)(6)(C) transaction" is an asset or stock acquisition, merger, or similar transaction involving a change in the Employer of the Employees of a trade or business.
(3)   The eligibility and service requirements outlined above ☐ are ☐ are not waived with respect to Employees employed on the Effective Date of this Plan. If these requirements are waived, such Employees shall become Participants in the Plan as of the Effective Date of the Plan.

52. Elective Deferrals:
  (a)   Amount of Elective Deferrals: A Participant may elect to have his Compensation reduced by the following percentage or amount per pay period, or for a specified pay period or periods, as designated in writing to the Plan Administrator:
    ☐ (1) An amount of at least _____% but not in excess of _____ % of a Participant's Compensation.
    ☐ (2) An amount of at least $_____ but not in excess of $_____ of a Participant's Compensation.
    ☐ (3) A percentage determined each year by the proprietor, partners, or board of directors of the Employer and communicated to the Participants on or before the pay period or periods in which such amount is deferred.
    Note: No Participant shall be permitted to have Elective Deferrals made under this Plan during any calendar year in excess of the dollar limitation contained in section 402(g) of the Code in effect at the beginning of such taxable year.
  (b)   Timing of Elective Deferrals:
    (1)   A Participant may elect to commence Elective Deferrals as of _____ (Date must be at least once each calendar year). Such election shall become effective as of the_____pay period following the pay period during which the Participant's election to commence elective Deferrals was made, or as soon as administratively feasible thereafter. Such election may not be made retroactively.
    (2)   The Participant will be permitted to change or discontinue the amount of his deferral election effective the beginning of the pay period coincident with or next following the "Change Date(s)" elected below:
      ☐ (A) First day of the first month of the Plan Year.
      ☐ (B) First day of the first or the seventh month of the Plan Year.
      ☐ (C) First day of the first, fourth, seventh and tenth months of the Plan Year.
      ☐ (D) First day of each month.
      ☐ (E) Each (at least annually):
    (3)   If a Participant elects to stop his Elective Deferrals at a time other than on a Change Date, he will be permitted to start again on:
      ☐ (A) The Change Date next following the date Elective Deferrals were stopped.
      ☐ (B) The Change Date following _____ after the Elective Deferrals were stopped.
  (c)   Bonus Payments:
    ☐ (1) A Participant may base Elective Deferrals on cash bonuses that at the Participant's election, may be contributed to the CODA or received by the Participant in cash.
    ☐ (2) A Participant shall be afforded a reasonable period to elect to defer amounts described in subsection (a) above. Such election shall become effective as of the _____(enter number) pay period following the pay period during which the Participant's election to make such Elective Deferrals was made, or as soon as administratively feasible thereafter.

53. Matching Contributions:
  (a)   The Employer will make Matching Contributions to the Plan on behalf of:
    ☐ (1) All Participants; or
    ☐ (2) All Participants who are Nonhighly Compensated Employees.
  (b)   Employees who terminate employment during the Plan Year with not more than 500 hours of service and who are not Employees as of the last day of the Plan Year ☐ shall ☐shall not receive an allocation of Employer Contributions.
  (c)   Such Participants in (a) above will receive Matching Contributions with respect to:
    ☐ (1) Elective Deferrals; and/or
    ☐ (2) Employee Contributions to the Plan.
  (d)   The Employer shall contribute on behalf of each Participant a Matching Contribution equal to:
    ☐ (1) _____ percent of the Participant's Elective Deferrals.
    ☐ (2) _____ percent of the Participant's Employee Contributions.
    ☐ (3) The Employer shall not match amounts provided in excess of $_____, or in excess of _____ percent, of the Participant's Compensation.
    ☐ (4) An amount, if any, determined by the Employer.
  (e)   If hardship distributions are permitted, Matching Contributions ☐will ☐will not be made with respect to Elective Deferrals withdrawn by the Plan Year end on a ☐ first in, first out basis ☐ last in, first out basis.
  (f)   Matching Contribution Compensation Period: Matching Contributions will be based on the following compensation period:
    ☐ weekly ☐ bi-weekly   ☐ quarterly ☐annual ☐ other:

FIGURE A-1   Adoption Agreement for a Qualfied Plan

54. (a) Vesting of Matching Contributions: Matching Contributions will be vested in accordance with the following vesting formula (choose one):
     ☐ (1) Nonforfeitable when made.
     ☐ (2) The Profit-Sharing Plan's general vesting formula, other than that for Elective Deferrals.
     ☐ (3) Other (Must be one listed under Item 36):
    (b) Forfeitures not used to restore Participant's Matching Account will be (choose one):
     ☐(1) Allocated in addition to Employer Contributions;
     ☐(2) Used to reduce otherwise required Employer Contributions; or
     ☐(3) Used to reduce Employer Matching Contributions and any remainder allocated in addition to the Employer Contributions.

55. Qualified Matching Contributions:
    (a) The Employer will make Qualified Matching Contributions to the Plan on behalf of:
     ☐ (1) All Participants; or
     ☐ (2) All Participants who are Nonhighly Compensated Employees.
    (b) Employees who terminate employment during the Plan Year with not more than 500 hours of service and who are not Employees as of the last day of the Plan Year ☐ shall ☐ shall not receive an allocation of Qualified Matching Contributions.
    (c) Such Participants in (a) above will receive Qualified Matching Contributions with respect to:
     ☐ (1) Elective Deferrals; and/or
     ☐ (2) Employee Contributions to the Plan.
    (d) The Employer shall contribute on behalf of each Participant a Qualified Matching Contribution equal to:
     ☐ (1) _____percent of the Participant's Elective Deferrals.
     ☐ (2) _____percent of the Participant's Employee Contributions.
     ☐ (3) The Employer shall not match amounts provided in excess of $_____, or in excess of____percent, of the Participant's Compensation.
     ☐ (4) An amount, if any, determined by the Employer.
    (e) If hardship distributions are permitted, Matching Contributions ☐will ☐will not be made with respect to Elective Deferrals withdrawn by the Plan Year end on a ☐ first in, first out basis ☐ last in, first out basis.
    (f) Matching Contribution Compensation Period: Matching Contributions will be based on the following compensation period: ☐ weekly ☐ bi-weekly ☐ quarterly ☐ annual ☐ other: _____

56. Qualified Nonelective Contributions:
    (a) The Employer ☐ shall ☐ shall not make Qualified Nonelective Contributions to the Plan. If the Employer does make such contributions to the Plan, then the amount of such contributions for each Plan Year shall be:
     ☐ (1) _____percent (not to exceed 15%) of the Compensation of all Participants eligible to share in the allocation.
     ☐ (2) _____percent of the net profits, but in no event more than $_____ for any Plan Year.
     ☐ (3) An amount, if any, determined by the Employer.
    (b) Employees who terminate employment during the Plan Year with not more than 500 hours of service and who are not Employees as of the last day of the Plan Year ☐ shall ☐ shall not receive an allocation of Qualified Nonelective Contributions.
    (c) The allocation of Qualified Nonelective Contributions shall be made to the accounts of:
     ☐ (1) All Participants; or
     ☐ (2) Only Nonhighly Compensated Participants.
    (d) The allocation of Qualified Nonelective Contributions shall be made:
     ☐ (1) In the ratio which each Participant's Compensation for the Plan Year bears to the total Compensation of all Participants for such Plan Year.
     ☐ (2) In the ratio which each Participant's Compensation not in excess of $_____ for the Plan Year bears to the total Compensation of all Participants not in excess of $_____ for such Plan Year.

57. Actual Deferral Percentage Test:
    (a) Qualified Matching Contributions and Qualified Nonelective Contributions may be taken into account as Elective Deferrals for purposes of calculating the Actual Deferral Percentage. In determining Elective Deferrals for the purpose of the ADP Test, the Employer shall include:
     ☐ (1) Qualified Matching Contributions; and/or
     ☐ (2) Qualified Nonelective Contributions.
    under this Plan or any other Plan of the Employer, as provided by regulations under the Code.
    (b) The amount of Qualified Matching Contributions made under Section 14.86 and taken into account as Elective Deferrals for purposes of calculating the Actual Deferral Percentage, subject to such other requirements as may be prescribed by the Secretary of the Treasury, shall be:
     ☐ (1) All such Qualified Matching Contributions; or
     ☐ (2) Such Qualified Matching Contributions that are needed to meet the Actual Deferral Percentage test in Section 15.04. (Box 2 can only be checked if the Employer has elected in Item #58(e) to use the Current Year Testing method.)
    (c) The amount of Qualified Nonelective Contributions made under 14.88 and taken into account as Elective Deferrals for purposes of calculating the Actual Deferral Percentages, subject to such other requirements as may be prescribed by the Secretary of the Treasury, shall be:
     ☐ (1) All such Qualified Nonelective Contributions; or

FIGURE A-1   Adoption Agreement for a Qualfied Plan

☐ (2) Such Qualified Nonelective Contributions that are needed to meet the Actual Deferral Percentage test stated in Section 14.71. (Box 2 can only be checked if the Employer has elected in Item 58(e) to use the Current Year Testing method.)

☐(d) If this is not a successor plan, then, if checked, for the first Plan Year this Plan permits any Participant to make Elective Deferrals, the ADP used in the ADP test for Participants who are Non-highly Compensated Employees shall be such first Plan Year's ADP. (Do not check this box if the Employer has elected in Item #58(e) to use the Current Year Testing method.)

58. Average Contribution Percentage Test:

(a) In computing the Average Contribution Percentage (ACP), the Employer shall take into account, and include as Contribution Percentage Amounts:

☐ (1) Elective Deferrals; or

☐ (2) Qualified Nonelective Contributions;

under this Plan or any other plan of the Employer, as provided by regulations.

(b) The amount of Elective Deferrals made under Section 14.77 and taken into account as Contribution Percentage Amounts for purposes of calculating the Average Contribution Percentage, subject to such other requirements as may be prescribed by the Secretary of the Treasury, shall be:

☐ (1) All such Elective Deferrals; or

☐ (2) Such Elective Deferrals that are needed to meet the Average Contribution Percentage test stated in Section 15.12. (Box 2 can only be checked if the Employer has elected in Item #58(e) to use the Current Year Testing method.)

(c) The amount of Qualified Nonelective Contributions that are made under Section 15.12, and taken into account as Contributions Percentage Amounts for purposes of calculating the Average Contribution Percentage, subject to such other requirements as may be prescribed by the Secretary of the Treasury, shall be:

☐(1) All such Qualified Nonelective Contributions; or

☐(2) Such Qualified Nonelective Contributions as are needed to meet the Average Contributions Percentage test stated in Section 14.88. (Box 2 can only be checked if the Employer has elected in Item#58(e) to use the Current Year Testing method.)

☐(d) If this is not a successor plan, then, if checked, for the first Plan Year this Plan permits any Participant to make Employee Contributions, provides for Matching Contributions or both, the ACP used in the ACP test for Participants who are Non-highly Compensated Employees shall be such first Plan Year's ACP. (Do not check this box if the Employer has elected in Item 58(e) to use the Current Year Testing method.)

☐(e) If checked, this Plan is using the Current Year Testing method for purposes of the ADP and ACP tests. (This box cannot be "unchecked" for a Plan Year unless (1) the Plan has been using the Current Year Testing method for the preceding 5 Plan Years, or, if lesser, the number of Plan Years the Plan has been in existence; or (2) the Plan otherwise meets one of the conditions specified in Notice 98-1 (or superseding guidance) for changing from the Current Year Testing method.)

59. Distributions of Excess Elective Deferrals: Participants who claim Excess Elective Deferrals for the preceding taxable year must submit their claims in writing to the Plan Administrator by _____ (Specify a date before April 15th).

60. Forfeitures of Excess Aggregate Contributions: Forfeitures of Excess Aggregate Contributions shall be:

☐ (a) Applied to reduce Employer Contributions for the Plan Year in which the excess arose, but allocated as in "b", below, to the extent the excess exceeds Employer contribution or the Employer has already contributed for such Plan Year; or

☐ (b) Allocated, after all other forfeitures under the Plan, to the Matching Contribution account of each non-highly compensated Employee who made Elective Deferrals or Employee Contributions in the ratio which each such Employee's Compensation for the Plan Year bears to the total Compensation of all such Employees for such Plan Year.

SAFE HARBOR CODA PROVISIONS

61. Safe Harbor CODA Provisions

(a) ADP Test Safe Harbor Contributions: In lieu of Basic Matching Contributions, the Employer will make the following contributions for the Plan Year [Select either or both]:

☐ (1) Enhanced Matching Contributions
The Employer will make Matching Contributions to the account of each Eligible Employee in an amount equal to the sum of:
(A) the Employee's Elective Deferrals that do not exceed ____ percent of the Employee's Compensation for the Plan Year plus
(B) ____ Percent of the Employee's Elective Deferrals that exceed ____ percent of the Employee's Compensation for the Plan Year and that do not exceed _____ Percent of the Employee's Compensation for the Plan Year.

FIGURE A-1   Adoption Agreement for a Qualfied Plan

☐(2) Safe Harbor Nonelective Contributions: The Employer will make a Safe Harbor Nonelective Contribution to the account of each Eligible Employee in an amount equal to 3 percent of the Employee's Compensation for the Plan Year, unless the Employer inserts a greater percentage here _____ %.

☐(b) If checked, the ADP Test Safe Harbor Contributions will be made to_____. [insert name of defined contribution plan of Employer]

62. Additional ACP Test Safe Harbor Matching Contributions

[NOTE: NO ADDITIONAL CONTRIBUTIONS ARE REQUIRED IN ORDER TO SATISFY THE REQUIREMENTS FOR A SAFE HARBOR CODA. HOWEVER, IF THE EMPLOYER DESIRES TO MAKE MATCHING CONTRIBUTIONS OTHER THAN BASIC OR ENHANCED MATCHING CONTRIBUTIONS, THEN COMPLETE THE FOLLOWING.]

For the Plan Year, the Employer will make ACP Test Safe Harbor Matching Contributions to the account of each Eligible Employee in the amount of [ELECT ONE]:

☐(a) _____ percent of the Employee's Elective Deferrals that do not exceed 6 percent of the Employee's Compensation for the Plan Year.

☐(b) _____ percent of the Employee's Elective Deferrals that do not exceed _____ percent of the Employee's Compensation for the Plan Year plus _____ percent of the Employee's Elective Deferrals thereafter, but no Matching Contributions will be made on Elective Deferrals that exceed 6 percent of Compensation. [THE NUMBER INSERTED IN THE THIRD BLANK CANNOT EXCEED THE NUMBER INSERTED IN THE FIRST BLANK.]

☐(c) the Employee's Elective Deferrals that do not exceed a percentage of the Employee's Compensation for the Plan Year. Such percentage is determined by the Employer for the year but in no event can exceed 4 percent of the Employee's Compensation.

63. Vesting of ACP Test Safe Harbor Matching Contributions: ACP Test Safe Harbor Matching Contributions will be vested in accordance with the following schedule (must be as favorable as those listed in Item #36):

Years of Service	Vested Percentage
Less than 1	
1	
2	_____(not less than 20%)
3	_____(not less than 40%)
4	_____(not less than 60%)
5	_____(not less than 80%)
6	100%

401(k) SIMPLE PROVISIONS

64. ☐ By checking this box the Employer elects to have the 401(k) SIMPLE Provisions described in Article XVII apply to the Plan. (This box may only be checked if the Plan uses a calendar-year Plan Year and the Employer is an Eligible Employer as defined in Section 17.02(b) of Article XVII. An amendment to have the 401(k) SIMPLE Provisions no longer apply is effective the next January.

65. The Nonelective Contribution described in Section 17.03(b)(2) of the Plan will be allocated to all Eligible Employees who received at least $ _____ [insert an amount less than or equal to $5,000] Compensation for the Year.

OVERRIDING LANGUAGE FOR MULTIPLE PLANS

66. If the Employer maintains or ever maintained another qualified plan (other than paired plan #01001, 01002, and 01004) in which any Participant in this Plan is (or was) a Participant or could become a Participant, the Employer must complete this section.

(a) If the Participant is covered under another qualified defined contribution plan maintained by the Employer, other than a master or prototype plan:
☐ The provisions of section 6.02 of Article VI will apply as if the other plan were a master or prototype plan.
☐ (provide the method under which the plans will limit total annual additions to the maximum permissible amount, and will properly reduce any excess amounts, in a manner that precludes employer discretion.)

(b) For Limitation Years beginning before January 1, 2000, if the Participant is or has ever been a Participant in a defined benefit plan maintained by the Employer: (Provide language which will satisfy the limitation for defined contribution plans in section 415(c) of the Code and for Limitation years beginning before January 1, 2000, the 1.0 limitation of section 415(e) of the Code).

FIGURE A-1   Adoption Agreement for a Qualfied Plan

RELIANCE ON OPINION LETTER

---

67. The adopting Employer may rely on an opinion letter issued by the Internal Revenue Service as evidence that the Plan is qualified under section 401 of the Internal Revenue Code except to the extent provided in Rev. Proc. 2000-20 , 2000-6 I.R.B. 553 and Announcement 2001-77, 2001-30 I.R.B. An Employer who has ever maintained or who later adopts any plan (including a welfare benefit fund, as defined in section 419(e) of the Code, which provides post-retirement medical benefits allocated to separate accounts for key employees, as defined in section 419A(d)(3) of the Code, or an individual medical account, as defined in section 415(l)(2) of the Code) in addition to this Plan may not rely on the opinion letter issued by the National Office of the Internal Revenue Service with respect to the requirements of sections 415 and 416. If the Employer who adopts or maintains multiple plans wishes to obtain reliance with respect to the requirements of sections 415 and 416, application for a determination letter must be made to Employee Plans Determinations of the Internal Revenue Service.

The employer may not rely on the opinion letter in certain other circumstances, which are specified in the opinion letter issued with respect to the Plan or in Revenue Procedure 2000-20 and Announcement 2001-77.

This Adoption Agreement may be used only in conjunction with basic Plan Document #01.

The Sponsor will inform the adopting Employer of any amendments it makes to the Plan or of its discontinuance or abandonment of the Plan.

NOTICE: Failure to properly complete this Adoption Agreement may result in disqualification of the Plan. The Employer's tax advisor should review the Plan and Trust and this Adoption Agreement prior to the Employer adopting such plan.

The undersigned Employer acknowledges receipt of a copy of the Plan and adopts such Plan this_____day of_____.

Name of Employer:_____   Name of Trustee:_____

Authorized Signature:_____   By: _____

Print Name/Title of Signer:_____   Print Name/Title of Signer:_____

Date: _____   Date: _____

FIGURE A-1   Adoption Agreement for a Qualfied Plan

RESTATEMENT EFFECTIVE DATES

Note: If this plan is not a restatement of any existing Plan, this item does not apply.

General Restatement Effective Dates:

Provision   Effective
Date

☐ (a) Not applicable. This is not an amendment and restatement.
☐ (b) The eligibility requirements of Item _____
☐ (c) The Employer Profit Sharing provisions of Item _____
☐ (d) The Vesting Formula of Item _____
☐ (e) In-Service
☐ (f) Loans
☐ (g) Definition of Required Beginning Date
☐ (h) Entry Date(s) of Item _____

401(k)/401(m) Effective Dates:

☐ (a) Amended to include:
                    ☐ Traditional 401(k);
       _____   ☐ Safe Harbor;

        ☐ Simple 401(k)
☐ (b) Commencement of Elective Deferrals   _____
           ☐ (c) Matching Contributions

☐ (d) Qualified Nonelective Contributions
☐ (e) Qualified Matching Contributions
☐ (f) In-Service Distributions
☐ (g) Financial Hardship
☐ (h) Hardship
☐ (i) Current Year Data election
☐ (j) Prior Year Data election
☐ (k) Top-Paid Group election

Note: The effective date(s) above may not be earlier than January 1, 1997 and not later than the last day of the Plan Year in which the Adoption Agreement is signed.

ATTACHMENT A

Name of Adopting Employer: _____

Address of Adopting Employer:

☐ Controlled Group; or ☐ Affiliated Service Group

List all "affiliated" employers with the above listed Employer.

Name	Address	EIN
1.		
2.		
3.		
4.		
5.		
6.		
7.		
8.		
9.		
10.		

FIGURE A-1   Adoption Agreement for a Qualfied Plan

Glossary

This glossary contains terms that you may encounter when investing in real estate with your retirement plans.

Acceleration clause Lenders usually write an acceleration clause into a borrower's loan documents, requiring that the balance be paid if payments are not timely or for other conditions in which the borrower is in breach of mortgage obligations.

Adoption agreement Part of a qualified plan. It establishes the terms and conditions under which the plan is adopted.

Ad valorem taxes Taxes applicable to a property in direct relationship to the property's value.

Advisory board A group of individuals, typically representatives of the major investors in a private equity or real estate fund, who advise the fund's general partner on various operational decisions such as conflicts of interest, asset valuation, and in some instances, new investments.

Agent The person or company acting on behalf of another person or entity to perform various business transactions, as established by a contract between the parties.

Alternative investments Includes investments in private equity, real estate, oil and gas, timberlands, and distressed debt. It also may include some varieties of hedge funds.

Amortization The process in which a borrower pays down a debt in accordance with a specific agreement with a lender.

Appraisal A formal process for establishing the market value of a property. It typically encompasses three approaches to value: discounted cash-flow analysis or capitalization of future cash flows (income approach), replacement-cost analysis (cost approach), and analysis of recent sales of comparable properties (sales-comparison approach). Appraisals often are conducted by third parties. In the United States, the Appraisal Institute provides a Member of the Appraisal Institute (MAI) designation to professional appraisers who have passed its certification requirements.

Assessed valuation Usually attributable to a taxing agency that provides a valuation of property for tax purposes. This assessed valuation might not represent a fair-market value or be an indication of comparable values.

Assignment A method of transferring property from one individual or corporation to another. The assignment can be for any property. Endorsements on a deed, stock certificates, or separate certificates can be used to document the transfer.

Assumption An obligation to pay an existing mortgage that is taken over by the buyer of a property. In an assumption, the buyer is substituted for the original obligor in the mortgage, who is released from any obligation relative to the mortgage. An assumption is not a "subject to" purchase; however, both are used to finance the sale of property.

Benchmarking Comparing returns of a portfolio with the returns of its peers. In private equity, fund performance is benchmarked against a sample of funds formed in the same year with the same investment focus.

Beneficiary A person for whose benefit property or funds are placed in trust or the recipient of an insurance fund or annuity. See also *IRA beneficiary.*

Binder An offer to purchase real estate, usually established through a preliminary agreement and sometimes supported by an earnest-money deposit from the buyer to the seller. The binder secures the right of the buyer on the agreed terms and conditions and a time period during which the agreed terms can be performed.

Blind pool A limited partnership that has been formed by investors pooling their capital for investment purposes. Virtually all private equity funds and the majority of private real estate funds are blind pools.

Bond In real estate, a written obligation secured by real estate and/or a note.

Bridge loan Temporary financing between major funding rounds for a private equity investment.

Business An activity where the profit motive is present and an economic activity is involved (IRS Publication 560).

Buy direction letter Letter provided to a plan administrator/custodian to initiate the purchase of an asset.

Buyout Acquisition financing for mature companies incorporating many strategies and structures. Small buyouts are fund sizes up to $500 million, medium buyouts are from $500 to $1,000 million, and large buyouts are above $1,000 million.

Capital The funds invested in a business. Investors can be individuals, partners, or shareholders. Generally, the intent of capital investments is to make a profit.

Capital expenditures The investment of cash or other property in a business, such as land, equipment, or other assets for business performance.

Cap rate For real estate investments, any rate of return used to convert income into value.

Carried interest Profit-sharing component of a general partners' compensation in a private equity or real estate limited partnership where profits typically are split 80/20 between the limited and general partners after return of capital.

Carryback A loan that is "carried back" by the seller of a property if the buyer does not have sufficient cash to make the purchase of the property entirely with cash. The seller carries back a note with specific terms and collateralizes this with the property, usually in first position.

Catch-up A common feature with many private equity and real estate funds where once the general partnership has achieved its preferential rate of return, the other, or limited, partners take all subsequent distributions until they have received their share of the designated carried interest to date.

Certificate of title Indicates that the seller has marketable title to a property. It is usually issued by a title company or other official method. When it is through a title company, the certificate of title is often insured. The issuer of the certificate is liable for defects owing to a negligent act. The protection offered is as good as the insurance backing the certificate.

Chain of title The history of ownership of a property, including its debts, liens, and other matters. In the United States, a chain of title usually is evidenced by recordation made at government agencies of the various states. In other countries, a chain of title may be evidenced by entries in records of government agencies' books.

Closed-end real estate fund A private real estate fund with a fixed fund size and a limited term, typically 8 to 15 years.

Closing costs Expenses assumed by the buyers and seller to consummate a real property purchase and sale transaction. These expenses include the costs of transfer of ownership and costs in addition to the sale price of the property, such as commissions (these also may be segregated from closing costs), appraisals, surveys, title fees, title insurance, recording fees, escrow fees, attorney's fees, documentary fees and stamps, and payoffs of existing encumbrances.

CMBS (Commercial Mortgage Backed Securities) Securitized form of commercial real estate debt in which multiple loans are placed in a pool, which typically secures multiple tranches of rated publicly traded bonds plus lower rated or unrated bonds with limited liquidity.

Coinvestment Investments alongside other partnerships in all types of private equity and private real estate, leveraging their due diligence, usually on a non-promoted basis. Coinvestment allocations lower the overall cost of private equity and real estate programs.

Committed capital Total capital committed to a fund by both the limited and general partners.

Common-law employee A common-law employee is any individual who, under common law, would have the status of an employee. A leased employee also can be a common-law employee (see *Leased employee)*. A common-law employee performs services for an employer who has the right to control and direct the results of the work and the way in which it is done; that is, the employer provides the employee's tools, materials, and workplace and can fire the employee. Common-law employees are not self-employed and cannot set up retirement plans for income from their work, even if that income is self-employment income for Social Security tax purposes. For example, common-law employees who are ministers, members of religious orders, full-time insurance salespeople, or U.S. citizens employed in the United States by foreign governments cannot set up retirement plans for their earnings from those employments, even though their earnings are treated as self-employment income.

However, an individual can be a common-law employee and a self-employed person as well (see *Self-employed individual*). For instance, an attorney can be a corporate common-law employee during regular working hours and also practice law in the evening as a self-employed person, or a minister employed by a congregation is a common-law employee and can declare the fees for performing marriages, baptisms, and other personal services as self-employment earnings for qualified plan purposes.

Compensation Compensation for plan allocations is the pay a participant receives for personal services for a year. This includes wages and salaries, fees for professional services, and other amounts received (cash or noncash) for personal services, such as commissions and tips, fringe benefits, and bonuses.

Composite IRR Aggregate internal rate of return across several funds where all cash flows are pooled as if from one investment, after which an IRR is calculated.

Consideration An inducement to enter into an agreement, usually in the form of money. Consideration also can consist of a property, right, interest, or other benefit to one party. Consideration is not required in some states, such as Louisiana.

Contribution An amount you pay into a plan for all those participating in the plan, including self-employed individuals. Each plan type has limits of how much can be contributed each year for a participant.

Custodian Designated individual or company who handles IRA or qualified plan assets and transactions. This entity must be approved by the IRS.

Debt financing Using a loan to pay for plan assets. This is subject to special rules regarding recourse and guarantees.

Deduction Plan contributions that you can subtract from gross income on your federal income tax return. Limits apply to the amount deductible.

Deed A written instrument that grants title to a property to an individual or entity. The deed may transfer title from one owner to another. The grantor of title is the seller or relinquishing party who coveys the property to a grantee. The grantee is the recipient of the property sold or relinquished in a transaction and is the person or entity to whom property is conveyed. Deeds generally provide an accurate description of the property conveyed. Deeds are used in the United States and many other countries. The contents of deeds may be prescribed by state laws. Third-party services may be used to ensure that the title is accurate and that other conditions of a transaction have been completed.

Deed of trust An instrument in which real property is provided as security for a debt. The lender is the beneficiary of the deed of trust. The trustee for a deed of trust holds the property in trust as an intermediary, securing the payment of an obligation to the lender, the beneficiary of the trust. The borrower transfers legal title to the trustee when the debt is incurred. Once the debt is satisfied, the trustee releases the title back to the borrower on notice from the beneficiary or lender. A note is generally the instrument that memorializes the debt. If the terms of the note are not satisfied, the trustee is instructed to sell the property to satisfy the terms of the note. In many states, the trustee may sell the property without judicial proceedings (nonjudicial foreclosure). IRAs and qualified plans may borrow on a nonrecourse basis from a lender who will make nonrecourse loans to an IRA or qualified plan. The lender will have recourse only to the property evidenced by the deed of trust.

Defined-benefit plan Any qualified plan that is not a defined-contribution plan. Contributions are based on actuarial computations of what is needed to provide determinable assets to each plan participant.

Defined-contribution plan A qualified plan for which the benefits are largely based on the amount contributed or deferred.

Depreciation The decrease in value of a property as it is used. Economic depreciation is the usability and utility of property for a specific purpose. For tax purposes, depreciation is the decrease and allowable adjustments to income over time using given formulas promulgated by the IRS. For IRAs and qualified plans, depreciation is used generally in the context of unrelated business income tax.

Development property A property investment involving substantial new construction, leading to the creation of a physical asset.

Disqualified person A person defined by the IRS who is disqualified from performing a transaction within an IRA or qualified plan. Common disqualified persons are spouses, lineal ascendants and descendants and their spouses, fiduciaries, and corporations, trusts, and so on that are owned by the plan participants.

Distressed debt Purchase of senior or junior debt instruments of a property, property portfolio, or a company or trade credits of a company when the borrower is in financial difficulty.

Distribution Withdrawals from a retirement account or plan. These are subject to IRS guidelines.

Dollar-weighted returns Private equity fund managers have a fixed investment commitment where inflows and outflows are at their sole discretion. Timing of cash flows should be factored into the returns because they are under the manager's control, using a discounted cash-flow method such as internal rate of return (IRR). Theoretically, time-weighted and dollar-weighted returns should be the same. This is true only when you calculate a periodic return every time there is a cash flow in or out of the portfolio; thus the value of the portfolio must be assessed at every cash flow. Frequent asset valuations are possible in public equities where liquid secondary markets post constantly changing prices by the minute. Private equity portfolios are revalued quarterly, so they cannot be repriced at every cash inflow or outflow. However, even quarterly valuations are only estimates because a liquidity event is at an unspecific date in the future, and immediate liquidity most likely is not possible. The private equity industry therefore uses an IRR calculation, which is by definition dollar-weighted, as a more exact measure of returns.

Drawdown schedule Plan for the transfer of funds from the limited partners' to the general partners' control. With most private equity and real estate funds, capital is called on an as-needed basis.

Due diligence The investigation and evaluation of a management team's characteristics, investment philosophy, and terms and conditions prior to committing capital to a fund. In terms of real estate investment, it is the detailed research of the property, the management team, and factors to ensure accuracy, completeness, and soundness.

Early-stage venture Fund investment strategy involving investing in a company whose business is operational but needs capital to hire employees, purchase equipment, develop products, and roll out sales and marketing programs.

Earnest money Funds deposited by a buyer to a seller to indicate an intent to purchase a real property at the time a sales agreement is consummated. Generally, the conditions of the application of an earnest-money deposit (sometimes referred to as a *good-faith deposit*) are governed by the agreement of sale or purchase. The funds usually are applied to the purchase when the sale is consummated and may be used as liquidating damages if conditions of the agreement requiring liquidated damages are provided for. This deposit is advanced to an escrow account by an IRA or qualified plan as part of the purchase direction to the trustee or custodian.

Economic life Time period in which a property provides a return to the owner. The economic life may be profitable, and when such profitability ceases, the economic life is fully depreciated for the specific purpose it was intended to produce a profit for (see also *Depreciation*). Changes in economic life take place when the purpose of the property or investment changes, sometimes as a result of outside forces, such as government regulations.

Employer A person for whom an individual performs or did perform any service, of whatever nature, as an employee. A sole proprietor is treated as his or her own employer for retirement plan purposes. However, a partner is not an employer for retirement plan purposes. The partnership is treated as the employer of each partner.

ERISA Employee Retirement Income Security Act of 1974, which more formally created the current use of qualified plans and IRAs. ERISA has been amended numerous times since then, notably providing for employee deferrals—401(k)s, Roth IRAs, and Roth 401(k)s.

Escrow agent Agent who assists with the administrative and some financial tasks of a real estate settlement.

Excess contribution A contribution made to an IRA or qualified plan that exceeds IRS limitations. These are subject to taxes.

Exit Sale of ownership or equity in a company or property investment either through a sale at the maximum return possible to a strategic buyer or a financial buyer or, in the case of a company, an IPO.

Fair-market value For real estate investments, the cash price that might reasonably be anticipated in a current sale after exposure to the open market for a reasonable period of time.

Fee disclosure Form provided when applying for an IRA or qualified plan that lists all the appropriate fees associated with the account.

Flipping Process of acquiring a property or asset and reselling, usually very quickly, at a profit. In many jurisdictions, the process of "buying and flipping" instantly violates the law.

Foreclosure Legal proceeding in which a bank or other secured creditor sells or repossesses a property owing to the owner's failure to meet the loan agreement. Some individuals and companies engage in the business of purchasing properties at foreclosure sales. Purchasing properties in foreclosure can be risky and should not be attempted by the uninformed.

Gross IRR Internal rate of return based on the performance of the investments, not taking into account management fees or carried interest.

Growth capital Development or expansion financing for mature companies.

Highly compensated employee An employee whose salary is greater than or equal to 10 percent of the employer's yearly wages. This is a disqualified person.

Holding period Amount of time an investment remains in a portfolio from initial financing to final liquidation.

Indirect rule An IRS guideline that states that a transaction that can be done directly should not be done indirectly. Violating this rule can be considered a prohibited transaction.

Individual (k) plan A qualified plan for business owners who have no employees.

Individual retirement account (IRA) An individual retirement arrangement that permits a wage earner to place pre- and posttax earnings into an account.

With a traditional IRA, the earnings are tax-free until mandatory distribution after reaching age 70½. Contributions are made within specific limits, and tax deductibility depends on the adjusted gross income of the wage earner. Earnings also may come from business income.

With a Roth IRA, you can contribute posttax money from wage earnings or business income to an account on which the earnings will not be taxed. Your income must fall within the limit set by the IRS to make contributions or convert funds from a traditional IRA. Distributions are not required. The Roth IRA must be established for five years to be fully eligible for nontax treatment of income.

Individual retirement annuity An individual retirement arrangement that permits a wage earner to invest in an insurance annuity on which the earnings are tax-free until withdrawn.

Individual retirement arrangement An arrangement established under the IRS Code that permits deductible and nondeductible contributions to be made by wage earners to certain accounts on which the earnings are tax deferred or tax-free.

In-kind contribution An asset contributed to an individual(k) account. The contribution must be at fair-market value and stay within contribution limits.

Interested party designation form A form provided when applying for an IRA or plan that allows the participant to designate a third party to receive information about the plan.

Interest on a note Percentage of the principal (original amount borrowed) to be paid periodically to the owner of an obligation. Interest may be due at the end of a note or periodically throughout the term of the note. Interest also may be paid on interest of the accrued but unpaid interest balance over time. This is usually referred to as *compound interest.*

Interim/implied IRR Return of a fund before the final termination date. Based on the internal rate of return calculated where the residual value of the fund is taken as the final cash outflow.

IPO (initial public offering) Sale or distribution of a stock of a portfolio company to the public for the first time.

IRA beneficiary Determining the required minimum distribution for an IRA beneficiary depends on whether the beneficiary is an individual or not. A trust cannot be a designated beneficiary of an IRA even if it is a named beneficiary under the IRS Code. However, the beneficiaries of a trust are treated as having been designated as beneficiaries if all the following are true:

1. The trust is a valid trust under state law or would be but for the fact that there is no corpus.
2. The trust is irrevocable or will, by its terms, become irrevocable on death of the owner.
3. The beneficiaries of the trust who are beneficiaries with respect to the trust's interest in the owner's benefit are identifiable from the trust instrument. This from the IRS.
4. The IRA trustee, custodian, or issuer has been provided with either a copy of the trust instrument with the agreement that if the trust instrument is amended, the administrator will be provided with a copy of the amendment within a reasonable time, or all of the following:
   - A list of all the beneficiaries of the trust (including contingent and remaindermen beneficiaries with a description of the conditions on their entitlement)

- Certification that, to the best of the owner's knowledge, the list is correct and complete and that the requirements of items 1, 2, and 3 above are met
- An agreement that if the trust instrument is amended at any time in the future, the owner will, within a reasonable time, provide to the IRA trustee, custodian, or issuer corrected certifications to the extent that the amendment changes any information previously certified
- An agreement to provide a copy of the trust instrument to the IRA trustee, custodian, or issuer on demand
- The deadline for providing the beneficiary documentation to the IRA trustee, custodian, or issuer is October 31 of the year following the year of the owner's death.

If the beneficiary of the trust is another trust and the preceding requirements for both trusts are met, the beneficiaries of the other trust are treated as having been designated as beneficiaries for purposes of determining the distribution period.

IRR (internal rate of return) Standard return calculation methodology in private equity and real estate. It is the discount rate that equates the net present value (NPV) of an investment's cash inflows with its cash outflows, or the annual effective compounded rate of return.

Joint-venture partnership Real estate investments in which an operator or developer teams with one or more financial partners to acquire and operate a property or a portfolio of properties.

LBO (leveraged buyout) Fund investment strategy involving the acquisition of a product or business from either a public or private company using a significant amount of debt and little or no equity.

Lead investor Investor in a syndicate that is the one that works most closely with management and negotiates on behalf of the other investors for the price and terms of an initial investment in a company, property, or subsequent financing round.

Leaseback option A business arrangement where an individual or company has an option on a property in which the property is simultaneously sold and leased back to the seller for use.

Leased employee A leased employee who is not your common-law employee generally must be treated as an employee for retirement plan purposes if the employee does all the following:

- Provides services to you under an agreement between you and a leasing organization
- Has performed services for you (or for you and related persons) substantially full time for at least one year
- Performs services under your primary direction or control

A leased employee is not treated as your employee if all the following conditions are met:

- Leased employees are not more than 20 percent of your non-highly compensated work force.
- The employee is covered under the leasing organization's qualified pension plan.
- The leasing organization's plan is a money purchase pension plan that allows for immediate participation, full and immediate vesting, and a nonintegrated employer contribution rate of at least 10 percent of compensation for each participant.

However, if the leased employee is your common-law employee, that employee is your employee for all purposes, regardless of any pension plan of the leasing organization.

Lender A third party who provides financing for a transaction. This can be a bank, mortgage broker, private lender, or other party.

Lien A charge or encumbrance against an item of property that secures the payment of a debt or some other obligation. Liens can be consensual (such as a mortgage) or nonconsensual (such as a tax lien).

Leveraged transaction Using borrowed funds for part of a purchase. Also known as *debt-financed transactions.*

Loan-to-cost Ratio of the current level of financing for a property investment to the cost basis for that investment.

Loan-to-value ratio Ratio of the current level of financing for a property investment to the fair-market value for that investment. This is a considered factor for obtaining debt financing.

Mezzanine Term is used differently in the real estate, venture, and buyout worlds. In real estate, it refers to subordinated debt financing, usually collateralized by a specific property or a portfolio of properties. In venture financing, it refers to the equity financing round just prior to an IPO, or it also can refer to middle- or late-stage venture financing. In buyouts, it refers to subordinated debt financing, usually with attached warrants, of more mature, stable, cash-flowing companies.

Money purchase plan Defined-contribution plan that has contributions based on an employee's compensation. Once a contribution level is established, it cannot be changed without IRS approval. This type of plan has not been used much since 2003.

Multiple Used either in reference to the multiple of cost a particular investment achieved (see *ROI*) or in reference to company valuation as a multiple of various income statement parameters.

Multistage venture Fund investment strategy targeting portfolio companies at various stages of development; sometimes referred to as *balanced stage.*

NCREIF Index A nationally recognized index that tracks the total return for a diversified basket of core property investments located in the United States.

Net earnings from self-employment Earned income from self-employment from a business in which your services materially helped to produce the income minus allowable business deductions. You also can have earned income from property your personal efforts helped to create, such as royalties from books or inventions. Earned income includes net earnings from selling or otherwise disposing of property, but it does not include capital gains. It includes income from licensing the use of property other than goodwill. Earned income includes amounts received for services by self-employed members of recognized religious sects opposed to Social Security benefits who are exempt from self-employment tax.

Net earnings include a partner's distributive share of partnership income or loss (other than separately stated items, such as capital gains and losses). It does not include income passed through to shareholders of S corporations. Guaranteed payments to limited partners are net earnings from self-employment if they are paid for services to or for the partnership. Distributions of other income or loss to limited partners are not net earnings from self-employment.

For the deduction limits, earned income is net earnings for personal services actually rendered to the business. You take into account the income tax deduction for one-half of self-employment tax and the deduction for contributions to the plan made on your behalf when figuring net earnings.

If you have more than one business, but only one has a retirement plan, only the earned income from that business is considered for that plan.

Net IRR Internal rate of return of a portfolio or fund, taking into account management fees and carried interest.

Nonrecourse loan Type of loan in which the only remedy available to the lender if the borrower defaults is to foreclose on the collateral. The borrower is not personally liable for repayment.

Note An instrument bearing legal evidence of debt. A note is signed by the borrower, who promises to pay a specified sum of money to the lender under the specified terms.

Open-end real estate fund A real estate fund with a long-term life during which new investors can be admitted on an ongoing basis, and existing investors can make contributions or withdrawals at their discretion. Open-end funds typically reinvest all operating and capital cash flows unless required to meet withdrawal requests.

Operating property A commercial property that is fully developed and is being operated to accommodate tenants.

Opportunistic real estate funds Real estate funds, typically structured as closed-end limited partnerships, that target higher risk strategies, such as development, redevelopment, lease up of vacant space, and distressed assets. Such funds usually use higher levels of leverage and have targeted net internal rates of return of 15 to 25 percent.

Option The right to purchase or lease property at a specific price within a certain time. Options vary greatly in construction depending on whether the option is on a stock, real estate, or a lease option.

Partner An individual who shares ownership of an unincorporated trade or business with one or more persons. For retirement plans, a partner is treated as an employee of the partnership.

Permitted investment Investment acceptable to a plan custodian or per IRS Disclosure Form 5305.

Personal property Property that is not real property, usually consisting of furniture, fixtures, and equipment not permanently attached to real property.

Plan administrator Party who performs administrative functions for an IRA or qualified plan.

Planned unit development (PUD) Usually consisting of mixed-use housing, which provides flexibility in design of a community. May be part of a master plan and may include zoning not provided under standard zoning ordinances.

Plan participant Owner of a plan or the person who opens the plan.

Private equity Professionally managed equity investments in the unregistered securities of private companies.

Private equity real estate Privately owned equity real estate investments that may be held directly or owned through participation in a professionally managed real estate fund.

Prohibited transaction Any improper use of an IRA or plan by the plan participant or any disqualified person.

Prohibited transaction exemption Request sent to the IRS to allow for a prohibited transaction in an extreme circumstance.

Qualified plan A plan approved by the IRS that allows tax-free or tax-deferred plans to be used for the purpose of retirement income. Contributions are made by an employee and an employer as applicable.

Quitclaim deed A deed that transfers the interest that the person quitclaiming the property has. Quitclaim deeds generally provide clear title. The buyer accepts all risks when accepting a quitclaim deed. This deed makes no warranty as to title and transfers the interest that the grantor had in the property. May be used for transactions involving IRAs and qualified plans where a buyer and seller have negotiated a transaction, provided that the parties are not disqualified under the IRS Code.

Real estate investment trust (REIT) A corporate real estate ownership vehicle created by the U.S. tax code that allows for a direct pass through of property income and capital gains to the company's shareholders, provided that the company makes annual distributions equal to 95 percent of its taxable income and that it meets certain tests with respect to the composition of its shareholders. A REIT must be composed of at least 100 members. The shares are freely transferable and are treated as partnership interests instead of corporations for tax purposes.

Real property Land, buildings, and any other permanently affixed attachment.

Redevelopment property A property investment that entails the substantial renovation of an existing building, which sometimes involves converting the property to a new use.

Reported value Value of the underlying investments in a private equity or real estate fund as reported by the general partner.

Residual value Remaining value of the equity in a fund, which is used to calculate interim performance before final fund liquidation, that is, cash and other assets net of liabilities plus the reported value of the remaining investments.

ROI (return on investment) Multiple of cost received on a particular investment at liquidation.

Sales agreement Contract in which a seller agrees to sell and a buyer agrees to buy a property subject to the specified terms and conditions. Also referred to as a *contract of sale, contract for purchase,* and *residential or commercial sales agreement.*

Secondary fund Fund that purchases private equity limited partnership interests or real estate interests in the secondary market.

Secondary market Market where securities can be bought and sold following their initial offering, such as the New York Stock Exchange or the Nasdaq. There is no formal secondary market for private equity or private real estate. However, some firms have raised capital to become market makers, purchasing private equity partnership interests from the original limited partners in the secondary market.

Security deposit Cash or anything of value provided to ensure payment of rent and proper discharge of rental agreements.

Security interest Interest in a property that secures the payment of an obligation or performance of a contract. Security interests can be filed with the appropriate government authorities for any property, real or personal.

Self-direction When used in context with IRAs and qualified plans, the ability of the account holders or plan participants to make their investment decisions. The extent to which self-direction is permitted is governed by the IRS Form 5305 disclosure for IRAs and the plan and trust document for qualified plans. IRA custodians or trustees can limit the extent to which an account holder may self-direct by including and excluding the plan options in the 5305 disclosure. Plan trustees can make the same limitations in the plan and trust documentation. Trustees can limit or expand such options on notifying the account holder or participant.

Self-employed individual An individual who is in business for himself or herself. Sole proprietors and partners are self-employed. Self-employment can include part-time work.

Not everyone who has net earnings from self-employment for Social Security tax purposes is self-employed for qualified plan purposes. See *Common-law employee* and *Net earnings from self-employment.*

Certain fishermen may be considered self-employed for setting up a qualified plan. See Publication 595, "Tax Highlights for Commercial Fishermen," for the rules used to determine whether fishermen are self-employed.

Sell direction letter Letter provided to a plan administrator/custodian to initiate the sale of an asset.

Servicer Third party who handles the administrative tasks of repaying debt financing.

Simplified employee pension (SEP) IRA A plan that allows an employer to make contributions to an employee's retirement plan without becoming involved in more complex arrangements. Contributions are made to a traditional IRA.

Sole proprietor An individual who is the sole owner of an unincorporated business. For retirement plans, a sole proprietor is treated as both an employer and an employee.

Special situations Opportunities that do not fit within an established category, usually targeting distressed companies.

Subject-to purchase Buying a property that is subject to an existing debt. In some cases, the loan on the property may be assumed by the buyer. In other cases, the lender accelerates the loan so that it can be paid off when the property is sold.

Subordinated debt Debt with inferior liquidation privileges to senior debt in case of a bankruptcy. Subordinated debt carries higher interest rates than senior debt to compensate for the added risk and typically has attached warrants or equity-conversion features.

Syndication Sharing of an investment among several private equity or real estate firms where the group is called the *syndicate*.

Tax lien certificate Documents the purchase of a tax obligation from a taxing authority. The tax obligation was previously unpaid by the property owner of record and then is sold to a private investor so that the taking authority can receive immediate income.

Third-party administrator Entity hired to perform the complex functions required on behalf of a trustee or custodian, such as contributions, deferrals, distributions, forfeitures, nondiscrimination, and tracking of employee accounts, as well as ensuring that all functions are carried out in accordance with the plan and trust. Many TPAs have actuaries on staff or on a consulting basis, particularly for defined-benefit plans.

TPAs usually are not involved with the investments but obtain the year-end reports from persons or companies involved with investments. TPAs usually prepare tax reports for the plan and provide them to the trustee or authorized person for signing.

Third-party record keepers Provide record keeping functions of all types for trustees or custodians of qualified plans and individual retirement arrangements.

TPRs may sign and submit unrelated business income tax returns to the IRS for the custodian or trustee.

Time-weighted return A time-weighted return is determined by calculating the rate of return between two or more periods, multiplying those returns together geometrically, and then taking the geometric mean of the result. For example: [(1.15 × 1.20 × 1.25)1/3] − 1 = 20 percent return. Time-weighted returns are an approximation of an IRR and usually are easier to calculate than the IRR. The term is a misnomer because it does not consider the time value of money but rather produces a return that does not penalize fund managers for timing decisions. The calculation treats a dollar distributed today the same as a dollar distributed 10 years ago. Time weighting was created to overcome the fact that the public securities manager has no control over clients' timing of the cash flow into or out of management owing to liquid secondary markets. The investment manager's performance is therefore measured strictly on the investment decisions made, not on the timing of cash flows.

Title report Report issued prior to a real estate settlement that provides a property description and informs the buyer and seller of any liens, lot adjustments, and so on that may affect the property in question.

Trustee The party that has control over the assets of an IRA or plan.

Unimproved property Land that is vacant and has no improvements that would make the property serve a useful purpose.

Unrelated business income tax (UBIT) Tax imposed by the IRS for any profit made on a debt-financed transaction in excess of $1,000.

Valuation method Policy guidelines to value the holdings in a fund. Venture funds hold the value of their portfolio companies at cost pending a write-up based on an arm's-length transaction or a write-down owing to impaired operations at the general partner's discretion. Buyout funds mark their portfolio companies to market based on discounted comparable public multiples at the general partner's discretion and usually under advisement of the advisory board. Real estate funds mark their property investments to market using a third party on an internal appraisal process, usually under advisement of the advisory board.

Value-added real estate fund Marketing term used to describe a broad range of real estate funds that engage in active strategies to create value in their underlying property investments, such as development, redevelopment, and lease-up of vacant space. Such funds target a broad range of returns and use modest to high levels of leverage.

Venture capital Financing and operational added value for younger start-up companies with high growth potential.

Vesting Portion of ownership of assets in a plan.

Warrant Option to purchase stock in a company over a specified period of time and under preset conditions.

Index

Hubert Bromma is the CEO of Entrust Administration, Inc. and speaks at real estate conferences worldwide. He is the author of *How to Invest in Real Estate and Pay Little or No Taxes*.